Morsels of
Musings

Morsels of Musings

When The Muse Sings

NISHU MATHUR

PARTRIDGE

A Penguin Random House Company

To order additional copies of this book, contact
Partridge India
000 800 10062 62
orders.india@partridgepublishing.com

www.partridgepublishing.com/india

CONTENTS

EARTH, AIR, WATER, FIRE
OF THE ELEMENTS

BONDS THAT TIE
LOVE POEMS

A WINDOW INTO INDIA

FOR THE INDIAN WOMEN

REFLECTIONS ON LIFE
DARKNESS AND LIGHT

ALL THAT MATTERS

TICKLES AND GIGGLES
ON THE LIGHTER SIDE

Poetess's Note

I consider myself as a 'poetess by chance'. Having stumbled upon the joy of words and verses, I took to writing a few years ago. My poetry may differ from many contemporary poets as I still pen in rhyme and rhythm. Very rarely do I write 'free verse'. My writings are mostly a celebration of life and the world around me. It is not often that I pen poetry of darkness. Not that I don't experience moments of 'darkness', it is simply that I prefer to focus on that which is beautiful. Then, I, as a poetess, am at the complete mercy of my muse. I follow the dictates of the lady who guides my quill.

In my first published collection of poems, I bring to you what I hold close to my heart. My poetry reflects life yet not all poems flow from personal experiences. Imagination, fantasy and reality weave into my words. Inspiration comes in many forms, from within me, nature, the cosmos, from other poets and poetry, from music and songs, even from the kitchen. The first few poems may give an insight into what poetry means to me.

In all that I write, I hope to bring joy in the heart of the reader and a smile.

I hope you enjoy these 'Morsels Of Musings'. Before you enter my 'poetic world', I share with you the thoughts and words of fellow poets and poetesses on my work. These poets are a few who have read my work and whose own work I have found inspiring.

Richard Gildea (UK)

'A 'Poet' in possession of such fertile mind; where each new dawn ushers in a veritable gamut of possibility. Her creative quill delights and astounds; with its imagery and comment providing a unique take on the world around us. This shining star amongst the firmament of expression entraps and enchants in equal measure.

Embracing the works of 'Nishu' exposes each reader to an inner beauty of singular kind'.

Maggie Pollock (Scotland)

'Nishu is an accomplished poet who writes with an open heart and within her writing we enter a wonderful world. A world, which shows all emotions. A world of love, hope, romance, excitement, laughter, also a world of beauty and tranquility when she writes of Mother Nature.

Nishu creates a vision of beauty in our mind as her words are a tapestry of colour and flow gently like a meandering stream. She is an excellent poet and her book will be an inspiration to all.'

Christine Shaw (United Kingdom)

'Step into the world of Nishu Mathur's poetry and you are greeted to a treat of vibrant colours, exotic places, tantalizing spices to tempt your taste-buds and aromatic smells. She has the ability to stir all the senses, whether writing of India and her culture, or whether she diversifies with her pen to write about matters of the heart, or the topical day to day. You will be guaranteed a sumptuous feast of reading. This anthology includes some wonderful poems. Too many to single out, but The Kashmiri Rug is a particular favourite.

Nishu is a gifted poet with a natural rhythm and flair for expression of the given word. She does not disappoint and you come away from her work feeling as though you have had the pick of the banquet, stimulated and satisfied.'

Sudarsan Damodar Prasad (India)

'When I read her, I wonder what is that appeals most about her poetry and touches my heart. Originality, awesome expression, uncanny ability to lie in the lap of nature and share her wonder, the deep lingering fragrance of human values and virtues, the haunting melody of a serenade, absorbing hum of a lover bee, the flutter of a humming bird's wings like the throb of a first love. Her poetry is a wonderful harmonious blend of all these and much more. Certainly and surely, uplifting is the last of its qualities and not its least.'

Nancy Crossland (USA)

'Nishu is a gifted poetess who gathers expressions of simple, every day occurrences and brings them to life to the reader. A versatile writer, she shows the true depth of character of the person she is focusing upon. From nature and the beauty of the world to humor as we take time to just laugh at ourselves. She is a poet for every age group and all who have the pleasure of reading her poetry will certainly be greatly entertained.'

Eddie Jepson (UK)

'Nishu is a talented poetess who writes with sincerity and compassion. Her poetry flows from the heart and leaves an impact on those who read her work. Her words reach the heart and set out what they are intended to do. Her poems are a joy to read.'

IF EVER I SING AS POETS HAVE

Word by word my notes I play,
I create a medley of thoughts,
Lyrics of my heart in what I say,
A song of my soul in phrases wrought.
Melody in verse and rhyme I see,
Into a realm I love or an escapade,
A haven it becomes in where I be,
Midst turquoise waters or dappled shade.

Art it is and a reflection too,
Of haunting beauty and reality,
A wisp of a dream or an opera true,
The rhythm of life and fantasy.
And there I be with my muse,
With laughter, tears, a thought to rue,
With notes in shades from reds to blues,
Through this I reach out to you.

And if ever I sing as poets have,
I shall sing of love, life and dreams as such,
Of the sun and moon, rains and storms,
Through my voice a heart to touch.

A TAPESTRY OF WORDS

A poem is a tapestry of words, a written art,
Dappled with feelings,
From the poet's heart.
It brushes with colors, bright or blurred,
With shadows that stalk the world.
Perhaps penned in joy or sorrow,
A song of a memory, of now or tomorrow.

It creates rhythm and music for the soul,
Some blues, reggae,
Some rock and roll.
It is of sunshine, daffodils, rain and stars,
It is of wastelands, horrors, warriors and wars.
A mirror it is of reality, of life,
Reflections of angst or mortal strife.
Or an escape to dreams, on wings of happiness,
Maybe of a mind,
Pained, repressed.

'Tis where an imagination stirs, inspires,
Where thoughts are flamed by a muse's fire.
It is a portal into a world of one's own,
Throbbing with people or at times alone.
It can tease a smile, sigh or cry,
Kindle reasoning, thoughts, a why.
It is what is read, or inferred,
As clear as crystal,
Or smudged and blurred.
A poem is of this world, yet beyond, divine,
Now and forever,
Scripted in time.

I SENT A TEARDROP TO MY MUSE

Once I caught a teardrop, I put it to good use,
I sealed it in a bottle and sent it to my Muse,
She wrote a little song, heart broken and forlorn,
And from one tiny tear, my first verse was born.
Once I caught a frown, I put it to good use,
I crumpled it like paper and sent it to my muse.
She smoothened all the furrows, gave it back to me,
And from my petty anger, she gently set me free.
Once I caught a smile, I put it to good use,
I gave it little wings and sent it to my muse . . .
With a twinkle in her eyes, I could hear her say,
With laughter in your heart, may you find your way.
Once I caught a thought, I put it to good use,
On my white winged horse, I flew right up to my Muse,
With a knowing smile, she held my eager hand,
She gave me a prayer, wisdom to understand.
And when, in gratitude, I thanked my feathered Muse,
She gave me a quill and said, ' Put it to good use'.

EARTH, AIR, WATER, FIRE
OF THE ELEMENTS

NICHE

It is the same garden that holds prickly rose bushes,
Healing basil and spritely marigolds.

It is here the bees fly, birds rest their wings,
It is here every morning the nightingale sings.
It is here the hare scampers, the squirrel scurries,
The snake slithers, the rodent hurries,
It is here the gecko hides, the worm crawls,
The bat flies when darkness falls.

In the mud and the dirt, the soil and the gravel,
In coarse little stones, smooth little pebbles,
In topaz skies, in waters azure,
In a lotus that blossoms in a world impure.
In the siesta of flowers, the fiesta of leaves,
In the dance of raindrops serenaded by a breeze.
In summer's golden glare, autumns russet finger,
In the green breath of spring, the white hand of winter.

Beauty in His creations, in every season.
In every color for a rainbow of reasons.
Each special and each rare,
Each in a bough or burrow,
Has a niche somewhere.

CAROUSEL

Carousel of clouds,
Contours of white in blue skies,
Merrily go round,
Up – down – up celebrating,
The carnival of morning.

THE LEAF

He floats in the air.
Swaying, prancing,
Twirled by the breeze,
Moving, dancing.
A dance in the air,
On hidden wings,
In love with the music,
Of the wind.
Graceful moves,
A performance brief,
Gently swirling,
The falling leaf.

For a moment on the ground,
He rests and stays,
Then another breath of wind
And swept away!

Flitting, floating,
Up and down,
Slowly in a ring,
Around and around.
Choreographed by the breeze,
In delight once more,
The breeze and the leaf . . .
The dance, encore!

COSMIC LATTE

Cerulean seas,
Raw umber russet rust mounts,
Deep fern forest green,
Cosmic latte universe,
Divine empyrean sheen.

THE – SUNLIGHT – CAPER

Behold those rays as they play,
Through the thicket of trees,
Trickles of beams midst the leaves,
In a caper, canter, free.

Sunlight ribbons in the air,
Amber streams be,
Rivulets of merry yellow,
No ebon ebony.

In fields in vales of velvet,
Swirl of sun on hills,
Spread of warmth in copper,
The walk of sun on stilts.

A – frolic on the mountains,
Through the cusp of clouds,
Here 'n there, hide 'n seek,
In and out, about.

Sun drops of gold in the blue,
In grace pirouette be,
Trending, blending, curling,
In the turquoise sea.

Oh, clasp a ray of sunshine,
Hold it close and tight,
In a hula hoop around you,
The caper of sunlight!

MARIGOLDS

A garden of marigolds, orange, yellow and rust,
Bright, soft and rich, touched with golden dust.
Quiet and regal, sun kissed and fair,
Basil – citrus fragrance that mellows the moist air.
A thousand smiling marigolds, a thousand smiling suns,
Sweet nectar and ambrosia, for nature's gentle ones.

Woven into garlands, yellow with tips of red,
Woven into memories with many words unsaid.

Love's hopes of an Indian bride, clad with marigold,
With dreams wrought 'n promises, her heart dearly holds.
Tearful farewell to soldiers who traverse through destiny's doors,
A garland weaved with love for those from across the seven shores.
And when the body is but a thought, as life greys and olds,
Wrapped in a hearse of love, their love, with weeping marigolds.
An offering so humble, yet flowers a Goddess wears,
Auguring celebrations, with a soul's heartfelt prayers.
Orange, yellow, rust, to love, to pray, to mourn,
Golden, sun kissed, blessed . . . marigolds that life adorn.

HAIKU (WATERMELON)

A burst of nectar,
Reprieve from flaming summer,
A seasonal tryst.

Tender fleshy chunks,
Sweetness dripping down the chin,
Mess in juicy fists.

Pink wedges red scoops,
Succulent water bites quench,
Drenched in happiness.

Slip, trip, dip into,
Crescents of watermelon,
Slices of pure bliss.

JUST A BEAUTIFUL DAY

A picture perfect day, blue skies, serene,
lilac rimmed clouds, a whimsy breeze.
Roses pink, ruby and rust,
fragrant in passion beside the Asoka tree.

Sun, playful with his auric sunshine,
basks in his own rays,
His aureate beams,
simmer, linger and stay.

A man with a basket of fruit hums his fare,
of oranges, grapes and avocados.
In no hurry with his medley of colour fusion,
whistling a merry tune he goes.

A sprinkler in a garden rains drops of water,
a little girl skips with her raven curls.
Her giggles voracious, her face animated,
midst confetti of rain that scuttles and whirls.

Soft music from the blue hills serenades in the distance,
mellifluous notes in resonance,
Moments to hold in the heart and eyes,
untouched yet . . . in blissful innocence.

THIS TOO SHALL PASS

I stand on the shore, my feet sinking in the sands,
My hair tousled wild in winds hustling hands,
Covering my face, veiling my eyes,
Distantly, I hear the seagulls, their yearning cries.
I grip firmer and hold myself tight,
In dusk's diminishing, dwindling twilight,
I watch the waves lunge at me,
Overwhelming, menacingly.
But as they race to the shore, reaching my feet,
They drench me, turn back, recede.

I see another wave, I yearn to move a step behind,
Fear and uncertainty fill my troubled mind,
But I still stand, stand my ground,
Unmindful of the sounds,
Of the winds and the waves,
In a trance, lost, nature's slave.
I nearly fall, my balance lost,
Taken by surprise, by waves tossed,
But I still stand, stand with unsteady feet,
Where the land and waters meet.

I, on the seashore, a speck, besides a sea so vast,
I know that each wave will rest, and it too shall pass.

INDIAN SUMMER

Strawberries, cherries,
Golden orange nectarine,
Fruit colours in blue skies,
Herald an Indian summer,
While white languid clouds float by.

COTTON CANDY CLOUDS

Through wisps of cotton candy clouds,
I saw the world, as it would seem to God,
Calm, serene, so much at peace,
The kind of world that he'd applaud.

Through tufts of cotton candy clouds,
I saw gentle strokes of divine hues,
No borders, no boundaries, no territories,
Just unending browns, greens and blues.

As I came closer to the land,
I saw tiny specks of human forms,
On the roads, in the field,
Sharing the sky, the sun that warms.

When my feet touched the ground,
I knew He wanted us to be one,
But I thought as I looked around,
What is it that we had done?

Then I wondered how He feels,
When He pauses to hear and see,
I wonder if He wonders,
'Why has man turned away from me?'

I wonder if He restless waits,
Sleepless, turning every night,
Waiting and wishing with all His heart,
Hoping that we could see His light.

And though He may not see us oft,
Praying head bowed, folded hands,
I wonder if He thinks at least,
That one-day, we might understand.

And I wonder if it gladdens His heart,
When He sees through His cotton candy clouds,
Kindness, love and compassion,
Somewhere, someone reaching out.

A MORNING WALK

The day turns but the night lingers,
The sky dark in the midst of mild winter,
The moon shy, the stars hidden,
The sun asleep, and not yet risen.

No sounds but the notes of early morn',
The soft subtle music of a still sleepy dawn.
Clouds flute through fields and trees,
Stirring life a symphony.

The air breathes fresh, no smoke nor smog,
The world fades faint in tufts of fog.
Fragrant grass, a thick carpet green,
Kissed by rain gods, it would seem.

Bliss and peace in tranquility,
The solitude in serenity.
I and me and just my thoughts,
On an early morning foggy walk.

THE LABURNUM

A yellow shower of a deciduous tree,
Sunshine flowers, wherever I see.
Streams of gold, in fields of green,
Eyes behold a summer queen.
Beauty groomed, a beaming head,
Blossoms bloom once leaves are shed.
Ornate bedecked, the brown red bark,
Lit up specks, though it be dark.
Cascading fall, feather light
Coloured pall by petals bright.
Healing touch lies within,
Summer's brush on the skin.
Ravishing gold a resplendent tree,
But in it's folds, poison be.

MY SUNRISE

This morning I woke up without worry's crease,
My mind and heart together in tranquil peace.
Dark clouds of doubts of yesterday,
Were left behind, castaway.
The morning sun, gentle, mellow,
Wrapped me in dawn's rosy glow.
Gingerly, touching my drowsy eyes,
And I welcomed him . . . my sunrise.
I felt his rays linger on my face,
Held by morning, in hope's embrace.
He brought with him, thoughts new,
Dreams yet to see, to come true,
I felt beautiful, alive. I felt strong,
I felt right, I could ne'er be wrong.
Happiness, glorious, undisguised,
This morn' I found in my sunrise.
A new beginning, a hopeful start.
This morn' I woke up with a sunrise in my heart.

THIS MORNING
ON AN ANGEL'S WINGS

A morning such as this,
Warms the heart so,
There could not have been a bluer sky,
Nor such a gentle glow.

Mist evanesced to bare a sun,
Shining on crimson trees,
Now scarlet flowers dance,
Stroked by a breeze.

With the rays of a morning Sol,
Flowers open wide,
Blossoming in the heat,
Of a cerise sunrise.

In the music of the dawn,
Where quiet are the words,
The breath of nature flutes,
In the songs of the birds.

On a morning such as this,
That heaven on earth brings,
Prayers fly to Him,
Riding on an angel's wings.

THE DANCE OF THE PEACOCK

As dark clouds thunder on a grey day,
Resounding across the arid plains,
I hear the loud cries of a bird,
It cuts across the rhythmic drumming of the clouds,
He's quiet for a moment, then I hear him again.

Through the trees I see him,
Royal, an electrifying metallic blue,
A peacock, stunning, strutting,
Fanning his train of feathers,
Eyespots of majesty, stroked with mossy hues.

He dances in a flamboyant display,
In spot light, as lightening flames the sky above,
Nonchalant, a blue crested head turns with pride,
His ornate train, shimmering, beckoning, to and fro,
His moves, a courtship ritual of love.

His iridescent trail woos in style,
A life of its own in its opaline shades.
Golden, blue, brown, green,
Colours of the earth, gloriously resplendent,
A gathered spectacle in his plumage.

As drops of rain touch the earth,
He is still high on the wings of romance,
His feathers spread for his mate,
In an extravagant array,
Quivering, glimmering a love dance.

HASNA HENA,
THE LADY OF THE NIGHT

In the still of the night when the sky is warm,
When a sultry moon sings a summer tune,
In the grip of darkness in raven shades,
As stars wink then shy away,
Lilac coloured blossoms bloom.

White, delicate, painted by Nature,
Tapering on tips with emerald leaves,
Each petal sings a season's song,
Elegant, dainty, bright and sweet,
The promise of light when darkness sweeps.

A fragrance that fills the heart,
Enchants, captive holds,
Fainter than jasmine, passion's rose,
Wayfarers rest to breathe in its lingering perfume,
Immersed in beauty as buds unfold.

A flower that lays quiet by the day,
Then in glory spreads in diminished light,
Withers, dies when winter strikes,
Hostile to cold climes, ice fingered tips,
Hasna hena, raat ki raani . . . 'The Lady Of The Night'.

PALASH
(The flame of the forest)

Olive green branches,
Flaunt vibrant crimson blossoms,
Seasonal bright blooms,
The fire of flaming palash,
Burns the dark contours of gloom.

SPRING SHOWERS

The sun chose not to shine today,
He stayed hidden behind dark dense clouds,
The sky a blanket of deep grey,
In defiance with thunder proud.
Yet the Bougainville gushed in delight,
Along the wall they crept, climbed,
Evergreen colours, resilient, alive,
Yellow, red, pink, entwined.
The wind was soft, just a breeze,
Forking leaves in her way,
Tantalising pre showers, a whisk, a tease,
Lingering, longing to stay.
The grass was green, the fields gold,
Mustard crops swept and swayed,
Heralding spring in emerald, saffron,
Hues in line, a relay.
Then it rained, drop-by-drop,
Drops in streams embraced,
I wished the rain wouldn't stop,
Life's droplets on my face.
I let the spring showers soak me,
Held beads of rain like I do,
Caught in the moment of a now and morrow,
Waiting for breath anew.

A FUCHSIA SUNSET

Fuchsia pink clouds,
Purple dappled across skies,
Dusky shadows queue.
Flaming orange orb descends,
Beyond waters midnight blue.

CHERRY BLOSSOMS

Rows and rows of trees,
coral pink and white,
Dressed in cherry blossoms,
ever so frail and light,
Clad in glorious beauty,
herald a season bright,
Pale fuchsias that
colour the darkest night.

Clouds of cheerful blossoms,
bowing gracefully,
Picture perfect, ethereal,
though their lives fleeting be,
Ephemeral, passing beauty,
lived in brevity,
Transience sung in folk songs
of man's mortality.

In delicate scattered beauty,
strength in fragility,
Flowers of death, soldiers pride,
inciting dignity.
Sakura etched in war
in a world's history,
Of sacrifice, war cries,
of blood fidelity.

Rows and rows of trees,
pale pink and white,
Showers of florid petals,
ever so dainty, light.
Cherish, revel in beauty,
while they breathe and be,
Ephemeral blossoms,
that bloom in brevity.

A SPRING MORNING

Twisting the limbs of cold winter,
Riding on winds that sing,
Winds a warm night breeze,
Singing the song of spring.

Dawn rises in early haste,
Roused from blissful dreams,
Steals away from the clasp of night,
Wrapped in rays that gleam.

The sun tingles in bright hues,
A splash of colours deploys,
Lilac clouds on a cruise,
Warm skies deep turquoise.

Birds flutter in a flurry of sounds,
The nightingale perches, woos,
Warblers hum their own songs,
Like lovers do.

Dahlias, pink and purple,
Touched by the hands of spring,
Primroses ablaze burst,
In rhapsodic riot tinged.

The world in golden radiance,
Buds and beings thrive,
Creation throbbing with life,
Nature awake, alive.

THE VENDOR AND HIS FARE

It is but February; the sun is already high,
A fiery orb, tangerine bright, torching the earth and sky,
Warm are the days and warm star clad, moonlit nights,
Heat rises, dusk or dawn . . . cool winds flee in flight.
Eager eyes seek relief, thirsty, parched lips sigh,
Though green, the earthy brown grows, seems barren, dry.

In balmy heat, he brings reprieve, with a welcome in his eyes,
Hands reach for what he sells, creases ease and smile.
A cart laden with coconuts, so tough though they would seem,
The vendor with his fare, tender coconuts, orange, green.
With a deft stroke, he knives the fruit, removes it's hard crown,
Tucking a straw in the well of water, in a moment, bliss rebounds.
Cool water of green palms, every little drop satiates,
Thirst quenched, lips soothed, the heat recedes, abates.
With another swoop, he scoops within, gathers the white meat,
Succulent, tender, creamy fruit, a taste of the tropics sweet.

THAT MYSTICAL PREDAWN HOUR

In that predawn hour,
In the midst of a hint of a mist,
In mystic magic when they say,
Gods and goddesses walk the earth,
I walk quietly.

Seen unseen,
Under a luminous, voluptuous moon,
That bathes the world in Aurelian glow,
Smiling at me from behind the dark arches of slumbering homes.

Watching me as I walk,
Marking and tracing the invisible footprints I make,
'Neath that pitch black sky,
When dawn is not far away.

The brightest of stars speak to me;
In sing song whispers,
Of dreams, desires I have whispered to them.

I walk besides green palms,
That stand proud and tall, like windmills,
Their earthy barks taut and strong.

A faint breeze plays with their leaves,
Dewdrops trip on their tips,
Gleaming in darkness.

The sun slowly rises,
Still a deep rosy pink from sleep,
Dawn stretches in languor,
Kissed by night,
Filling the fading night sky,
With soft cerise blushes,
Delicate tangerine touches,
With light,
And blissful arrays of,
Peaceful blues.

The world awakens drowsily,
To the music of the birds,
Ganesha hymns,
The early morning chanting,
The soothing strings of a sitar and,
Ragas in hypnotic tones from the temple.

THE HEAT IS ON! A SUMMER CALL

The temperatures are rising,
It's not really surprising,
I hear summer call.
Winter has gone hiding,
Spring trotting and riding,
Far is russet fall.

There's a breeze so enticing,
A bed of blooms inviting,
Palms are growing tall.
Emerald leaves are dancing,
Roses red romancing,
In warm colours all.

The birds are now singing,
Sweet notes cooing, ringing,
In a silver squall.
But . . . mosquitoes are biting,
The flies are not dieting,
And there are lizards on the wall.

The frogs are out hopping,
Bugs are window shopping,
In a green mall.
Geckos are fighting,
A camouflaged rioting,
A best buddy brawl.

A few reptile sightings,
Now isn't that exciting?
See them crawl.
No longer are they hiding,
But mates they're deciding,
How they sprawl.
The heat with fire igniting,
Inciting and delighting ,
Hear babies bawl.
The temperatures are rising,
It's not really surprising,
I hear summer call!

SUMMER SPLASH

Red watermelons, pale musk melons,
Luscious lychees creamy sway,
Purple plums, pastel pears,
Whisk summers heat away.

Crimson cherries, pink guavas,
A yellow mango sunrise,
Scarlet crushed pomegranates,
Splash a summer surprise.

Tender coconuts, jambul blues,
Peaches nectar, sweet limes,
Vineyard grapes shimmering gold,
Simmering summer wine.

Medley of the colours of life,
Songs warm breezes sing,
Season's tropical fusions,
Succour in summer's wings.
As searing heat waves rise,
Respite a season brings,
Gentle relief from summer herself,
In nature's own offerings.

A CATNAP

A purr-fect day it is today,
For a catnap.
A languid sonorous noon,
Summer under a hat.

Stretched snug in the garden,
Beneath the tree,
With dancing butterflies,
The birds and the bees.

The warmth of the Sun,
Wrapped around fingers,
On drowsy toes,
Sleep lingers.

The song of wind chimes,
A melange in the breeze,
The red gulmohar brushing,
With rustling leaves.

The scent of red roses,
White jasmine,
Adrift in the air,
Fragrance within.

White lustrous clouds,
In blue skies,
The wings of an eagle,
Caught in the eyes.

A lull . . . a lullaby,
The heart at ease,
Thoughts fade,
The mind at peace.

In the folds of early noon,
Eyelids close,
Far from the humdrum,
A purr-fect doze.

SUNSHINE

Sunshine days,
Amber rays,
Waves soft and warm,

Prancing beams,
Sing to me,
Over is the storm.

Through clouds a burst,
Aurelian dust,
Razzle – dazzle light,

Flaming skies,
Kiss the earth,
Over is the night.

Posies heave,
On emerald leaves,
Petals peek a bloom,

Fluttering, flapping,
Humming, tapping,
The koel coos a tune.

Vanilla clouds,
Puffed and proud,
At dawn's own behest,

Turquoise dome,
Ablaze with light,
The day is on a quest.

As winds parade,
A serenade,
Music sweet at play.

The skies unfold,
A golden stole,
May the sun shine on you today.

A WALK IN THE SUMMER RAIN

At last heavens relented,
The skies opened, it poured,
Drip – drop, splash – slosh,
Rollicking – drops – a – roar!

At last clouds covered the orb,
Banished brazen rays,
The searing summer sun tucked,
Sunshine breezed away!

At last the palms danced,
To the rhythm of the winds,
Whirling arms of frolicking green,
In abandon, in a spin!

At last the orchids laughed,
Roses bloomed again,
Oh how the marigolds smiled,
It rained and it rained and it rained!

And I a feint form,
'Neath heavens waterfalls,
Chasing rolling winds,
In the midst of it all.

The skin cleansed, the heart calm,
Each drop heavens kiss,
The scent of earth in rain,
The soul replenished.

A potpourri of flowers aired,
Blown with moist gales,
Champa, chameli, gulab,
Elixir inhaled.

With the song of the koel,
A heart's melody unchained,
Magic unleashed from skies on earth,
A walk in the summer rain!

SEVEN HUES TOGETHER IN A BOW

A bridge it is between earth and heaven,
gentle beauty that kisses the sky,
embracing land with its arms of colours seven,
it is down to earth yet reaches high.

Hope it promises within its arched form,
peace and calm as life is renewed,
over is thunder and rain drenched storms,
glimmer golden rays on a canopy blue.

Man smiles and warms to its many coloured glow,
each colour is of life, each colour diverse,
yet together the colours stand, seven hues in a bow,
sheer poetry it is, a metaphor in verse.

A rainbow is what the eyes see and behold,
enchanting magic as nature often does,
and dear it is for our hearts to hold,
for isn't there and may there always be . . .
a rainbow within us.

THOUGH I LOVE THE RAIN

Though I love those dark clouds,
and though I love the rain,
how it brightened my heart,
when the sun came out again.

The sky a sea of tranquility,
as peaceful as could be,
calm I felt when those gentle rays,
rested upon me.

I'm sure I heard the roses laugh,
saw carnations turn a richer hue,
how could they but not smile,
upon a sky so cobalt blue.

I saw the lake ripple,
silver with copper streams,
glistening with quiet joy,
how it glimmered and beamed.

Though I love those dark clouds,
and I love the rain . . . I do,
but how my heart gladdened today,
for I can do with sunshine too.

I hope the sun lingers a while,
shining through sheesham trees,
for I love the way his rays rested,
so softly upon me.

THE SONG OF THE FOREST

I walked past blue mountains,
Along the crystal stream,
I ambled deep into the forest,
In a mist of emerald green.
Beams of light pirouetted,
Sol's fire of purity,
Birds preened their wings,
In a shade of serenity.
Whispers rustled in the air,
Earth, water gushed,
A hymn of wind in symphony,
In harmony though hushed.
Midst the song of the forest,
A murmur in the breeze,
My soul, engulfed in silence,
Yet singing . . . at peace.
I stood on firm earthen ground,
At one with trees and ferns,
Knowing it's from here I come,
And here I will return.

MONSOON MOMENTS

A stream of steady raindrops,
Drizzling clouds never cease,
Along the roof, climbing creepers,
On beds of strewn Bougainville leaves.

The breeze becomes restless,
And whirls into a gust,
Running through clustered, arching trees.
Headlong in a rush.

The drizzle turns a torrent,
A dance on rooftops,
Drops of rain gather to meet,
Puddles of water crop.

Beaming faces glean, glisten,
Young feet splash in mud,
Cloaked in a wave of water,
Slip, slosh, thud.

Paper boats in a fist of rain,
Weather the raging storm,
Bubbles of children drenched in joy,
Indelible memories form.

A nose pressed against a window,
Peers through the glass,
Born of rain . . . water dunes,
The roads lap and splash.

Hair drenched soaking wet,
Strands clustered cling,
Clothes drape hugging close,
Drops roll on the skin.

A 'dhaba' lures with its warmth,
Hands lingering hold,
Basil flavoured cups of tea,
Lovers nestle close.

Huddled beneath a parapet,
A sundry blend of folks,
Eye the gorging slate grey skies,
Ruing their rain coats.

Across the road . . . a tug of war,
But chances stand thin,
A man with his umbrella,
Its swept away by the wind.

Upside down, inside out,
A merry chase is on,
A canopy that somersaults,
Up close and it's gone!

THE GULMOHAR TREE

The gulmohar tree,
In flamboyant love of life,
A burst of colour and cheer,
Bright vermillion,
Under his glorious crimson spread,
A shaded, blissful haven.

Children reach for his branches,
Clasping, holding,
Climbing, swinging,
Chasing, laughing,
Under a bright shower of scarlet petals,
Of life and love, of beauty, of hearts and heat,
Blooms of a warm Indian summer.

In flames, his vibrant burning crown,
His canopy, flaunting festive tangerine blossoms,
Crinkled teasing petals,
One upright,
Of innocence touched in white,
Splashed with feisty red,
Celebrating and anticipating,
A celebration of love and life,
In anticipation,
Reaching for dark clouds of rain.

Serenading with the music of the monsoons,
Moist leaves of the gulmohar glisten and gleam,
With wind and water, in gentle rhythm.
Raindrops nestle for a moment,
Before sliding, slipping,
On damp, satiated earth.
Strewn bright with scattered rich orange petals,
Of the gulmohar, drenched and soaked.

ETERNAL SUMMER

While hearts resonate with sounds of autumn,
No dry rustling leaves I hear or see,
No footfalls of fall I welcome,
It is an eternal summer for me.
No icy winds my cheeks brush,
No leaves orange and rust be,
No august autumn's rising blush,
Colours the canopy of green trees.

Roses, hibiscus, pink, red and white,
Gulmohars, Chitras, in warmth breathe,
Sheltered from frost's cold blight,
Weaved and wrought in summer's wreathe.
And while birds, content, sing of summer time,
I long for the magic of autumn's clime.

DANCING IN THE RAIN

Let sleet grey skies darken,
And the wind vanes spin insane,
Let it drizzle, let it pour, let it pound,
I'll be dancing in the rain.

Let thunder sound its drums,
Raw, loud untamed,
Let raindrops pelt their music,
Upon the window pane.

Let lightening flash in silver,
Across night's ebon mane,
Those twisted streaks of light,
I'll be dancing in the rain.

Let clouds fill and burst,
Let heavens touch the plains,
Let water meet the rivers,
Merry on musty lanes.

Let the wind sing its song,
Leaves hum a refrain,
Trees, like me, we'll be dancing,
We'll be dancing in the rain.

A POLKA IN THE AIR

On a narrow winding road,
Where winds rushed to be,
I came across a canopy,
A canopy of merry trees,
In love's eagerness,
Forward they bent and leaned.
Colouring tawny eyes,
With shades of wooded green.
Branches interlocked,
Arms raised and swayed,
Across the winding path,
Where lost travellers strayed.
Winds breezed with joy,
When arms sought their pairs,
Reaching out across the road,
A polka in the air.

The morning summer sun,
Peered through the trees,
Just a wisp, a glimpse,
Through the impregnable canopy.
Beneath it I walked,
In sheltered, shielded reprieve,
Caressed ever so gently,
By the touch of falling leaves.

THE JACARANDA TREE

There she stands the jacaranda tree,
In sunshine rays of morning gold,
Wrapped in a lavender stole,
Of flowers so gracefully.

Her blossoms are of enchanting hue,
A whiff heaven sent,
Mauve dipped in nature's scent,
In a shower of cascading blue.

A floral spread she spreads in style,
A canopy surreal,
Dancing in a summer smile,
As florets bow and kneel.

In gentle lilac her beauty glows,
Enamoured is the wind,
In dulcet tones, the wind she sings,
As through the leaves she blows.

Blooms in delicate violet whisper,
A secret no one knows,
Rustling quiet, hushed and low,
Can you hear the murmur?

THOUGH IT'S A COLD GREY FOGGY DAY

Noses have become bright red,
A sneeze away and they flow,
Clouds of fog outside the window,
It may as well snow.

Hands and feet are like ice,
Wrinkled, crinkled are fingers,
Fists are turned into heater balls,
Pushing back winter.

The sun is intent on sleep and rest,
He winks and would rather not rise,
Bundle up says the weather man,
I look up at the sky.

Not today, the cold will rattle,
Though winds may raise a storm,
It may pellet and freeze,
But the heart stays ever warm.

I'll paint the cold, lackluster sky in colours,
With warm sunflowers, roses and iris blue,
Write across in burnished bold gold,
Love, peace and happiness to you.

LET IT SNOW

It's cold outside but warm within,
Rose candles golden glow,
With you here right beside me,
Let winter say hello.

The fire's all cracklin', blazin',
On the wall play love's shadows,
Contours of time a racin',
Let winter winds bellow.

Your eyes like stars a twinklin',
I'm lit from my head to toes,
The chords of my heart a jinglin',
Let cold winds blusterin' blow.

Hearts alive, all hustlin',
And the music turned so low,
Whispers of sweet nothings,
As winter steals the show.

A white night beaut' unfurlin',
Snowflakes dance so slow,
Twirlin', scufflin', swirlin',
Let it snow, let it snow, let it snow!

HAIKU (WHITE WINTER THROUGH WINTER)

White winter frost breathes,
Untouched sparkling fire lit hearths,
Glow mistletoe wreathes.

Spring soft serenades,
A parade of budding buds,
Veiled fog further fades.

Summer hot saunters,
Mosaic of colour blossoms,
Sweet vibrant santons.

Falls red robust rush,
Russet colours prelude to,
White winter's frost touch.

OF BEAUTY WARY BE

Leafless trees encased in glass, frozen water's rush,
Fragile ice that traces it with a delicate chiseling brush.
Fields, plains of freezing rain, ice that glides on ice,
Sparkling wrapped artefacts, winter storms surprise.

Lakes a sheath of glimmering glints, shining showcase silver,
'neath the clinking gleaming ice, life awakes 'n quivers.
Little droplets fall to freeze, cold with warmth meets,
Sliding, slick, slippery . . . crystal clear sheets.

An artist's world, an art glazed, an art redefined.
Tread careful, 'tween life and death, a fine thin line.
Perfect strokes of an air brush . . . beauty winter bequeaths,
But of beauty wary be, for dangers lurk beneath.

A JANUARY GARDEN

Red roses flutter in the wind,
Palms dance with open arms,
Hibiscus pinker than before,
Has blushed deep in the sun's warmth.

Bougainville in yellow flaunt their hues,
Marigolds russet won't be subdued,
Beams of the sun bless,
Wands of gold from a velvet blue.

Ivory jasmine sashay in white,
Petals arrayed in sweet perfume,
Raat ki rani roused alive,
When at night she sees the moon.

Passion fruit afloat a throne,
Carnations whisper, none quiet,
In tangerine, purple, fuchsias,
Gerberas in riot.

Basil basks in mud baked pots,
Creepers climb in curved vines,
Petunias twirl and whirl in violet,
Swaying with wind chimes.

Blossoms play on emerald leaves,
How they love the January breeze,
Nature spins sweet florals,
With scented shades that please.

LOVE THOSE NIGHTS

Love those nights when my head touches the pillow,
And my eyes are closed quick by gentle sleep,
No sounds come near me,
In peace and quiet, I rest deep.

Love those nights when nothing ails,
But so tired I be,
The world, moon, stars, the sun,
Sleep the night right beside me.

No tossing, nor fluffing the pillow,
No fretting, nor restless turns,
No yarns to spin or untie,
Beyond desires that yearn to burn.

No lightening frightening I see,
Nor roars of loud thunder heard,
No far-fetched flights of fantasy,
To distant worlds when light blurs.

No thoughts that come knock on doors,
No lingering doubts that call,
No nagging fears threaten,
Wearing down comfort's wall.

In the arms of restful sleep,
Where weariness bids adieu,
Dreams, nightmares, a forgotten haze,
Where life breathes life anew.

Love those nights when I lay in bed,
When mind and heart are not astir,
When my head but touches the pillow,
And to sleep I surrender.

EVANESCENCE

The sun sets beyond the sea,
Birds homeward fly,
The moon peers from between the hills,
Stars light the skies.

Night writes her own songs,
Lyrics in ebony ink,
Fireflies dance midair,
Stars dip and wink.

Darkness colours the world around,
With raven tones of night,
Silhouettes of trees loom tall,
Swaying shadows in starlight.

Waves break upon the coast,
On cragged shores grey,
Sweeping grains of sand with them,
The day is washed away.

The world lulls to restful sleep,
Thoughts disperse and leave,
Reality in evanescence,
It's time for dreams to weave.

BEAUTY FOR BEAUTY'S SAKE

Entrapped, enchanted and enamoured,
By a vision ethereal sublime,
My heart stops for a moment,
As do the hands of time.

Stars, twinkling, adorn,
A night as dark can be,
The beauty of the full moon,
The glistening magic of the sea.

Irradiance resplendent,
Her glory gently grows,
An orange, golden, globe,
That in the waters, silver glows.

With long silken fingers,
Her rays with tides play,
In the folds of rippling waters,
Tickling the merry Bay.

Glimmering silver waves,
Reach for the moon,
They swish and sashay,
Dancing to natures tune.

Breathless I watch,
Spellbound I partake,
Absorbed, immersed in beauty,
Just beauty, for beauty's sake.

ON A CRESCENT MOON

Last night, I rode the crescent moon, cradled in her arch,
And she carried me away to a world apart.

I flew beyond the flowering trees, the towering hills, clad in black,
The plateaus and the plains, beyond rugged snow capped peaks,
Brown hardy mountains with no green.
I saw the deep blue sea . . . surging dark,
With silhouettes of shadows unseen.

I met Sleep on the way. She seemed in much haste,
She had a rendezvous with a pair of eyes, they wouldn't close,
She said with a sigh.

I saw Despair, hovering around earth's realms,
Feeding on darkness, gaining strength, with a hope to overwhelm.

I met the twins, the twain,
Nightmare and Dream,
Eager to reign,
Antipodal yet alike,
Riding on tinsel moon beams.

Then I saw Love, embellished with the stars of Hope,
And beautiful was she,
As only she could be.
In her presence, much faded,
Despair cowered,
Nightmare cringed,
But Dream brightened,
And Sleep winked.

I saw the fabric of the cosmos,
Stitched with threads of Love,
Occasional stitches undone,
Little gaps that came along,
A tear here, there,
But a fabric unparalleled and strong.

THIS NIGHT . . . THIS NIGHT WAS MADE FOR ME

A raven blue sky,
floats of smoky clouds,
smudged in pink and violet.

Sterling stars scattered,
on the canvas of time.

An argent moon with rays of gold,
craving and spreading,
to be a celestial whole.

Midnight fragrances,
florals mingle, with a rain spray,
scents borne by the wind,
steal my breath away.

Palms bend low with grace,
tender leaves are rippled,
by a summer breeze.

In the light of darkness,
surreal beauty, bliss,
heaven this must be,

This night I know,
this night,
was made for me.

"MOONSTRUCK"

In the evening sky,
He hung in celestial glory,
I thought he came early.

As the blue paled,
He became brighter.

Luminous, white and bold,
I loved him dearly.
I held him in my hands and heart,
Cupped his fullness,
In my eyes.

He moved with me,
I watched captivated.
I stood in his golden light,
And beauty,
Soaking in silver slivers,
Into my soul from my skin.

Now he lives in me,
And I in him.

BEFORE 'TIS NIGHT

Before the sun sets, and the dusk dawns,
Before the night gives way to a twilight morn,
On blue waters in the oceans, I'll set my heart a sail,
For it's wept so . . . from red, run a pallid pale.

Before the new sun rises, the moon fades away,
Before the stars wane in the glory of the day,
I'll give my heart, for the earth to keep,
And in her deep folds, it could sigh and weep.

Before the moon smiles, before moonbeams fall,
Before stars wink, murmur and call,
I'll set my heart free to soar in the sky,
For then, when it rains, it could hide and cry.

Before the day is done, and the night arrives,
Before a thousand dreams come throbbing alive,
Before fireflies illuminate, the world alight,
I'll let go of my heart, before 'tis night.

And before the blue sky turns to midnight dark,
Before distant runs the rainbow's arc,
Before my eyes close, yet again torn apart,
I'll find myself another heart.

A CELESTIAL CELEBRATION

Each night such beauty unfurls,
tonight the moon has turned a pearl.

No clouds of purple, no violet tinge,
no smoky grey, no hues of pink.

Just deep strokes of midnight ink,
with silver stars that quiver and wink.

Cream and ivory my eyes see,
on a sky of blue ebony.

Moonbeams in a dance slow,
sprinkling moon dust as they go.

Encompassed in golden rings,
such charm and joy Celeste brings.

'Heaven's cloth' aglow agate,
tonight must be a night,
angels celebrate.

GARDENING

Today I am gardening my life,
I'll root out worrisome weeds,
Those thoughts that trouble me,
Cast them aside, those I'd never need.

I'll cut the grass of discontent,
Layer it even, soft, pleasing, green, sweet,
Smoothen the furrows,
So I can run content, bare feet.

I'll water seeds planted with love,
Of friends made this year,
Friendships that bloomed,
That make life worth living and dear.

I'll welcome butterflies,
Make homes for nesting birds,
With them, taste sun's ambrosia,
Soar and see the world.

I'll bask in the rainbow of colours,
Of blossoms brilliant bright,
And keep them sheltered,
When they sleep at night.

I'll capture the essence,
Of roses, jasmines and lilies,
Place them in a jar,
For fragrant memories.

I'll love, rest and spend more time,
Under the shade of the family tree,
Cherish every moment, every minute,
'Neath its precious canopy.

And I'll buy new saplings,
Sow them all carefully in a row.
Of hopes, promises to me and mine,
And tend to them, make them grow.

THE MUSIC OF THE MOUNTAINS, THE HIMALAYAS

Here, the ceiling is a deep cobalt blue,
white clouds embrace mountains,
barren jagged peaks meet skies,

A forest of proud sentinels stand tall,
looking on meadows green,
entangled twines.

Sparkling crystal lakes,
startle with their depth,
in hues of green and pacific,

Untouched land casts a spell on,
travellers, poets, artists,
lovers, dreamers and mystics.

In summer, beds of marigolds and daisies,
white orchids, blue poppies,
stretch in a yawning morning mist,

Silver fir, spruce, blue pine,
soak droplets of rain,
drenched in a monsoon kiss.

Autumn with her wick of amber,
lights candles,
flames the leaves in russet shades,

Winter landscapes the green in white,
a canvas of snow,
over meadows and glades.

The valley opens her heart with warmth,
flakes melt into olive,
buds with zephyr spring,

Frosted ice clad lakes melt,
flora blossoms in wilderness,
in virgin blues and pink.

The scents of nature, the sounds of earth,
the sights of paradise,

The music of the mountains,
sings to the soul,
and plays in the eyes.

CLOUDS HAVE MORE
THAN A SILVER LINING

The sky oft becomes dark and thunders,
there are clouds as grey as can be,
but behind those clouds waits the sun,
quietly and patiently.

Of course it will rain and pour,
clouds will rumble, clash and roar,
but they will not forever last,
those dark clouds will come to pass.

These clouds are not just rimmed in silver,
look up close, with hope behold,
for those black threatening clouds,
are lined with the brightest gold.

ON THE BEACH AND IN THE SKY

I greet the morning sun with Surya Namaskar,
Hands folded, a prayer.
Arms stretch above as I reach to touch him;
The body quietly arches,
In compliance with the laws of the cosmos.
Sunrays drench me with golden light,
I stand on grains of sand,
Feeling each grain with my breath.
Ripples of water caress my feet, now soaking wet,
So gentle, an ocean's touch when the waters are calm.

Unrestrained joy as I feel the white frothy sea,
The blueness of the waves rushes into my heart.
They push their way deep inside of me,
I inhale the scent of the ocean,
Hear the whisper of the waves, the murmur of shells.
A light breeze encircles me, wraps me tight,
Carries me lightly on her wings.

I rise with the sunrise,
In a cosmic dance with the twirl of spheres,
My heart and I merge with the moment,
The now.
The here, in peace.

THE LAST SUNSET

I saw the sun set in all glory,
So beautiful and so clear,
A ball of flaming pink,
In a blink it disappeared.

How swiftly the day went by,
So quickly time flies,
When it's time to turn and go,
How hard to say goodbye.

Photos frame in memories,
Each heart beat can be heard,
On a trampoline of feelings,
Still stand the words.

When moments carve a niche,
Why do eyes turn shy,
When it's time to turn and go,
Why must the soul cry?

HAIKU (RAIN)

Whimsy wind waltzes,
Wading in waves of water,
Washed with wet whispers.

Rotund raindrops roll,
Rambunctious rendezvous,
Racing revelry.

Sun seizes the storm,
Simmering satin sunbeams,
Shine in satiety.

Chrysanthemums cheer,
Carnations in carnival,
Coloured calypso.

THE SPLENDOUR IN THE GRASS

Turning on wheels, running past trees,
Few moments to pause and breathe,
Inhale the mist from lavender fields,
Bathe in the green from leaves.
The sun will shine, rain will fall,
Summer will heat and burn,
Fall will flame, white winter unfurl,
Spring with blooms return.
White clouds will float, birds hum,
But eyes shut, ears not tuned,
Untouched by the brush of butterflies wings,
Mute voices, still, won't croon.
Gardens will pale, no fragrance of jasmine,
That bursts and heals from within,
Heart shut, mind shuttered,
No petals will kiss the skin.

Oh, slow down in the mad rush.
Pause with the gross, the crass,
Eyes open, heart beating;
Breathe in the splendour in the grass.

BONDS THAT TIE
LOVE POEMS

FOOTPRINTS IN THE SAND

There is nothing like for a thirsty voice water clear and sweet,
A loaf of bread for a hungry man and his misery would retreat.
There is nothing like for tired eyes a night of gentle sleep,
Nothing like for a weary body the comfort of slumber deep.

There is nothing like for an unsteady voice the call of a friend,
No broken heart that a friend's love cannot heal or mend.
There is nothing more warming than a twinkle in tiny eyes,
And nothing more stirring than a new born's hushed cries.
There is nothing like for a tearful child his mother's warm hold,
Or the wisdom of generations through his father told.

There is nothing like for a bruised soul the balm of gentle words,
The miracle of a kind voice in deep recesses heard.
There is nothing like for a battered soul the warmth of a smile,
The promise of a tomorrow though it may take a while.
There is nothing like for a broken soul the touch of a helping hand,
Gestures never washed away . . . eternal footprints in the sand.

ON GIVING

True giving,
Is more than giving fragrances and flowers,
Artifacts, knick knacks,
That gather dust on ageing shelves,
True giving,
Lies not in a mere showering of gifts,
But in giving, as one gives a bit of one's self.

ASKS

Sweet words, that sweeter sound,
A pledge of vows, hopes abound,
Whispers promise a love beyond,
Sealed with a kiss, but a fragile bond.

Hands held in a warm grasp,
Smiles, soft, lingering, bask,
But ties are more than mere words,
Asks that often go unheard.

Care, understanding, sacrifice,
An unsaid quiet compromise,
Appreciation, deep respect,
Each the other would reflect.

Fragile bonds, fragile ties,
Sealed with empty words that lie,
Crumble like a pack of cards,
A game played by frivolous hearts.

LOVE'S CULINARY STEW

Unlike the broth that wicked witches brew,
Of frogs, lizard legs, a spiders webbed face,
I have cooked loves culinary stew,
Of affection, smiles and a warm embrace.
I have taken large measures of my love,
From deep within my heart, well meaning, true,
Layered with prayers made to Him above,
Blended earnest heart felt wishes for you.
From an Indian summer, poured sunshine,
The colour of rainbows to brighten days,
A promised friendship simmered over time,
Should bitter dark thunderstorms come your way.
Sprinkled laughter, hope and joy over this,
I now serve (garnished) with a hug and kiss.

WHY? JUST BECAUSE

Just because a prayer isn't answered
Why would I stop to pray?

Just because there was no sun
Why wouldn't it shine today?
Just because tears wet a morn
Why would the noon cry?
Just because clouds spanned across
Why wouldn't the eve be dry?
Just because the sky was grey
Why wouldn't it turn a blue?

And just because a dream faded
Why wouldn't the others come true?

THOSE MOMENTS

My heart loves when the sun,
flares with a copper glow,
when dusk drapes and falls,
a curtain of indigo.

My heart dances when it rains,
then when it's gold with shine,
for when dark clouds gather,
I see a silver line.

My heart is young with flowers,
that in wilderness grow,
a forest of quaint scents,
that in the winds do blow,

My heart smiles with the stars,
shining atop pine trees,
the glint of a cosmic moon,
cradled in the sea.

My heart rides on the crest,
of waves on the ocean floor,
that kisses a pearl rare,
and floats it on the shore.

My heart loves these moments,
that I with nature be,
but none, more splendid, more beautiful,
than those of you with me.

THE GREATEST GIFT OF ALL

I may not have the most beautiful face in the world,
a face that'd launch a thousand ships,
no precious tresses, no hourglass figure,
nor those coveted lucky lips.

I may not have intelligence extraordinaire,
no doctorate in philosophy,
no glittering, intellectual accolades,
those golden showcase trophies.

I may not have the riches of the world,
nor own castles sky high,
no treasures, no royal bounty,
no princess nor Empress I.

I may never be in the headlines,
nor on television seen,
my eager piquant face won't cover,
the pages of star kissed magazines.

So not a genius, rich or famous,
I am but a face in the crowd,
yet I walk on sunshine,
and my head's up in the clouds.

For I know I have the greatest gift of all,
I have been blessed from above,
more precious than anything else,
hearts that dearly love.

THROUGH HER EYES

She saw beauty in an orange orb, in grey skies, in thunderclouds, in rain,
And though he looked high and low for beauty, his search was all in vain.
She saw beauty in a blade of grass, in barks of trees, in willowy green
plains,
He saw the drying grass, the weeds, the yellow leaves and turned away in
disdain.
She saw beauty in a puddle, in choppy waters, sinking shifting sands,
He saw coarse murky grains, menacing dark waves breaking barren lands.
She saw beauty in the light of a dying candle, a flickering lamp, a glow
with grace,
He saw growing darkness, looming shadows where beauty had no face.

She felt beauty in the touch of raindrops; the beams of the afternoon sun,
Heard her in tinkling laughter, in whistling winds, in the daily humdrum.
But he could neither feel, nor hear, nor touch, nor see beauty go by
How could he . . . he'd closed his heart . . . And he wouldn't even try.

If the world, through her eyes, but for a moment he could see,
There would never a dearth of beauty in his eyes ever be.

THE FLORIST

She sells flowers in little bunches,
Sweet fragrances that please,
Delicate sepals of life,
That softly speak.

Bouquets of living colours,
Petals of inspiration,
Roses, chrysanthemums,
Daisies, carnations.

Accent blossoms, gerberas,
Lilies smiling in myriad hues,
Sunflowers a darling yellow,
Vibrant orchids in splendour blue.

With her touch, beauty breathes,
Glorious blossoms thrive,
Delicately arranged,
Floral expressions come alive.

For new love that slowly blooms,
For confessions yet to be said,
The finest of her finest,
She ribbons roses dark rich red.

Fond good health thoughts,
Through florals expressed,
She'll wrap with gentle care,
With loves tenderness impress.

She'll weave wreathes and garlands,
Blends of wistful white, blues, pinks,
For memories left behind,
Now distant imprints.

In sweet scents, she colours days, months, years,
Walks alone each night when she is done,
Back home, no florid fragrance fills her senses,
To colour her world there is no one.

KARMIC CONNECTION

Not knowing . . . . you and I,
Beyond the planes of physical realm,
An unsaid bond, a baffling tie,
Holds hearts close, overwhelms.
Magnetic pull, an iron hold,
Spanning several seasons,
A bond strong, love in it's folds,
Defying logic and reason.
In your hands I place my hand,
Of yours but a reflection,
Writ beyond the laws of land,
The tug of Karmic connection.

Not knowing . . . you and I,
Beyond tangible reality,
Unanswered how, unanswered why,
Unfathomable affinity.
Spanning distance, spanning time,
Across the universe,
Like hearts, like minds,
That quietly converse.
In your thoughts I see my own,
Of my mind a reflection,
Knowing I was never alone . . .
The pull of a Karmic connection.

WHAT ARE DREAMS MADE OF

Dreams are made of chocolate huts,
With burgundy windows, cherry knob doors,
Sweet icing on cream layered roofs,
Almond – walnut – caramel floors.

Dreams are made of iris and jasmine,
Jacarandas lined in purple rows,
Tree blossoms in clustered cobs,
Petals that dance like a ballerina's toes.

Dreams are made of fern green forests,
Oakwood trees that cast a spell,
A gossamer web of magic and charm,
The music of clinking coins in a wishing well.

Dreams are made of cerulean skies,
Contrails of clouds in ivory snow,
Violet mystic misty mountains,
A tangerine orb riding a rainbow.

Dreams are made of romance laced nights,
A golden peach vanilla moon,
Venus lighting, igniting, love's fire,
The silhouette of love in rain soaked June.

Dreams are made of turquoise seas,
Calm waters stroked by gentle waves,
Or enticed by the charm of a midsummer night,
Waters that heavenly Cynthia craves.

Dreams are made of silk and satin,
Dappled with reds, greens and blues,
But the dreams that I love to dream the most,
Are all the dreams made of you.

THE LANGUAGE OF LOVE

'Tis not always spelled in letters,
'Tis not always said in words,
'Tis not always sung in notes,
Loud enough to be heard.
'Tis not always writ in sands,
Nor frosted window panes,
'Nor engraved on precious stones,
Ornate jewelled chains.
'Tis not always spilled on paper,
Nor carved on barks of trees,
The language of love,
'Tis more than words can be.
It might ne'er be understood,
Or perhaps deftly read,
For much of what is love,
May pass away unsaid.
But 'tis there in tenderness,
Longing wistful eyes,
A heart that lights up,
Every moment love comes by.
'Tis there in a gentle hold,
A shoulder kind enough,
Caring thoughts that sail you through,
Choppy seas, weathers rough.
'Tis colouring you a happy pink,
When the world grey's a blue,
Love is more than words can say,
Love is more than 'I love you'.

WHEN I FALL IN LOVE
I'D THOUGHT

When I fall in love I'd thought,
There'd be much I'd want to say,
But when I fell so deep in love,
No words would come my way.

How strange it was, so I thought,
I'd sing of it night and day,
But when so deep I fell in love,
Words were swept away.

'Twas writ clear in my heart,
'Twas there in my eyes to see,
'Twas in my thoughts, my mind,
But no words came to me.

I dreamt dreams that'd tease my morn,
The moon and stars in my eyes,
When so deep I fell in love.
I quiet and tongue-tied.

Just as well my love was seen,
The heart, the blush, the sweeping red,
For by the time I would've found some words,
My dear love would have fled.

THOUGHTS OF YOU

The sky is still dark, though its early morn,
Dark rain clouds, no trace of blue,
As I walk through wind swept lanes,
The winds but bring thoughts of you.

I hear the distant roar of thunder,
Lightning flashes as if on cue,
And as the wind picks up a storm,
All I do is think of you.

The first few drops of rain that fall,
Drops that breathe life anew,
And as the trees spring to life,
My heart's alive with thoughts of you.

As I stand in the falling rain,
Soaked to the skin, through and through,
The wind that sweeps through verdant lanes,
Will carry my love and thoughts to you.

VINTAGE WINE

Rich golden peaches,
Bottled,
In vintage wine,

Heady, sweet,
Overwhelming,
This dear love of mine.

BUT HOW CAN IT BE . . . ?

Turquoise waters entrap,
sunlight that pirouettes.

Golden specks dance within, spin.
Waves sashay.
Sunlight still captive within the folds.
It's all aquamarine marigold.

Some say heaven is this,
in beauty, in peace and bliss,
in copper tawny rays, on a sea deep blue.

But how can it be my love?
When I know,
Heaven is you.

CAUGHT A GLITTER

I caught a glitter of falling stars.
One by one, I sprinkled them on the frothy bay.
So you could pick and wish a dream,
When darkness turned to cerise day.
I asked the wanton moon to cast her glow,
Richer in gold,
Beyond the raven night.
Beams of halcyon to hold that wish,
Ribbon it safe till sunlight.

I asked the orchid purple clouds of dark,
Floating, loaming, dipping,
Kissing the ebon blue,
To carry that wish,
Within their folds,
At dusk, dawn,
Till it came true.

A TINY SEED OF LOVE WAS SOWN

It was when our eyes first met . . . the knowing look,
the glance that locked on a breezy spring day,
when April rain danced in a ring of whirls,
and dark windy clouds music played.

It was when you first whispered my name,
your voice just a moment away,
when the colours of a thousand flowers burst,
when the summer sun smiled its winged rays.

It was when you first held my hand,
the warm touch in your tender hold,
wrapping me in moonlit russet dreams,
a world of scarlet autumns gold.

It was when we first danced,
beside the blushing fire that amber glowed,
crimson steps with hearts of bliss,
as winter spread her cape of snow.

It was at dawn, at noon, at dusk,
I swept, lost, tossed and blown,
you, my love, did take my breath away,
and a tiny seed of love was sown.

A HEARTBEAT AWAY

As you sleep, I watch over you,
I see you quietly smile,
In bliss in a world of your own,
Cushioned from life's trials.
Wrapped in warm dreams content,
I can only pray,
May the sun shine on you,
Brightening, lighting the way.

Forever in my heart I know,
I'll hold you close to me,
Bubble wrap you fine and tight,
For most special, precious you be.
The joys of life be always yours,
Smile night and day,
But should you ever need me my love,
I'm just a heartbeat away.

SO MUCH LOVE

A lifetime isn't enough for loving you.
I have so much love to give.
And if I could,
I would my love,
To love you,
Another life I'd live.

DREAM A LITTLE DREAM

When night sings a lullaby,
And Venus cradles the world,
When eyes are lulled by moonbeams,
Dream a little dream.

When feisty fireflies fly,
Clouds of luminous lights,
When the stillness of the night gleams,
Dream a little dream.

When I'm a thousand miles away,
Far for you to hold,
When loneliness overwhelming seems,
Dream a little dream.

When at night, you lay your heart,
And thoughts uncrowded seem,
Think of me, with you I'll be,
Dream a little dream of me.

ALWAYS

Through hard days and easy ones,
Through upheavals that test.
Through sorrows and happinesss,
Through comforts that bless.
Through clouds and rainbows,
Through rain and the sun,
Through uneven roads,
That through destiny run.
Through tunnels of darkness,
Through a valley of light.
Through demons in the mind,
That a heart always fights.
Through the smiles and the laughter,
Through the pain and the strife.
Through the ups and the downs,
In this journey called life.
Through the good and the bad,
Whatever time accrues,
You know . . . I'm always,
And,
I'll always be there for you.

ON 'LOVING YOU'

I thought of a thousand reasons,
why I shouldn't love you,
I made a tally,
a little score.
I thought,
and I thought,
and I thought,
only to know,
how now,
I love you even more.

IN THE RED THAT LIES WITHIN

Love comes unannounced a quaint blue moon's day,
When you least expect it then, and takes your breath away,
It never calls, no knocking, waiting for sunrise,
Tip toes, quiet, sudden, whispers a surprise.
Love feels no spring, no fall, nor the whims of clime,
No dawn nor twilight, no pendulum of time,
No seasons of life it knows, no bars of age,
A heart in love is free, wings beyond a cage.
Love heeds no borders, no tell tale lines at all,
No religious creed, no man made custom walls,
It breezes through barriers, through flesh, bone and skin,
Resting deep in the heart, in the red that lies within.

When love comes, they say, it sweeps you off your feet;
A true blessing love is, when love is yours to keep.

A WHISPER OF YOU

Stardust sprinkled,
crescent smile,
sliver of a moon,
upon an isle,
star clad nights,
a deep sapphire,
purple clouds,
breathe fire,
ivory wings,
on ebony coasts,
violet dreams,
forever float,
serenade of winds,
wind through,
whispering my love,
a whisper of you.

BETWEEN THE SILHOUETTES

She'd veil her eyes, cloak her thoughts,
And slip into the night,
Cross the greens to meet her love,
'Neath the night skylight.

In stealth and quiet, love concealed,
Midst murmurs of the pines,
The forest hid her rustling form,
In darkness, clandestine.

She'd wait between the silhouettes,
Hold her breath, then calm,
To breathe again in happiness,
In her lover's arms.

And as he came, in eager haste,
Through the shifting mist,
His breath so warm, he called her name,
With love awaited tryst.

Stars sparked a tinsel bright
Moonbeams waved a dance,
The clouds afloat in their eyes,
The lovers in a trance.

Her dreams alive, hopes adrift,
That time would never end,
The sun would steal a longer wink,
Night would not relent.

For there she was with her love,
Where she did belong,
Her world, her heart . . . it felt so right,
Then how could this be wrong.

But as the night gave way to day,
The blush of early morn,
The two'd melt away like mist,
As night with the dawn.

PERHAPS WE'LL MEET AGAIN

Perhaps our paths were meant to cross,
Share a tear or smile,
Hold the other's hand with care,
And walk in stride a while.

But then you chose a different road,
One I could not tread,
I saw you turn then walk away,
My words were left unsaid.

As you walk your own way,
However you choose to go,
Always a friend you'll be,
Forever I hope you know.

May the good Lord stand by you,
In sunshine or in rain,
Perhaps our paths were meant to cross,
Perhaps they'll cross again.

SOMETIMES

Sometimes it's best to love,
love . . . the only way you can,
in love's different splendored shades,
that across the spectrum span.

Sometimes it's best to give,
give . . . the only way you know,
in thoughts, in smiles, kind acts,
for never wasted they go.

Sometimes it's best to carry on,
loving and giving as only you know how,
for that is the only way to a sweeter tomorrow,
and a happier now.

FOOTPRINTS OF LOVE

On every eyelash rests a dream,
and more intense it turns,
when eyes close at the end of day,
when stars light and burn.

With every heartbeat,
beats a beat, so close to your own,
in rhythm with your heart,
'tis never ever alone.

With every step that you may take,
uncertain or unsure,
with you I walk,
footprints of love,
true, strong and pure.

LINGERING FRAGRANCE

The fragrance of love lingers in the air,
like the scent of white jasmine,
like the fragrance of rain soaked earth,
whisked by a summer wind.
It stays day and night in the mind,
like incense, in thoughts, it spreads,
forever the scent of roses,
forever a scent in red.
It fills the senses like heady ittar,
though but a dab on the skin,
in what is felt and touched,
makes the senses spin.

It lingers forever in the heart,
a fragrant melody, one so true,
forever it sings and plays,
a song of love and you.

A LOVE POEM?

I thought I would write of love, love,
But then I faced a wall, a block,
My quill stood still in time,
While the clock went on tick tock.
I thought I would write of passion,
That makes one dance on toes,
But my quill stayed quiet still,
It wouldn't spill ink or flow.
I thought I would write of romance,
With all the right beats in the groove,
But my quill stopped mid air,
It didn't want to write or move.
So I lay my quill aside,
And gave poetry a miss,
I left the pages empty, love,
And sealed them with a kiss.

IT IS ALWAYS RAINING YOU

Dark skies when blue fades,
clouds burst in happiness,
a cascade of drops,
soaking earth,
a rosary of shimmering beads,
crystal droplets dance in puddles,
peer through glass windows,
tapping on roof tops that slant,
thatched homes that drip,
on twigs and branches,
on ruby tangerine roses and sunny marigolds,
settling in scarlet and auburn crevices,
on emerald leaves and blades of satin green grass,
glistening like drops of morning dew,
in the midst of the gentle splash of the rain,
there you are,
it is always raining you.

THE SPELL OF YOUR LOVE

The sun rises in your eyes and sets at your feet,
The sun at your mercy my love, in your heart beat.

The roses bloom with your smile, wither with your tears,
The magic that is you my love, your breath warm, sweet.

The birds sing in ecstasy, in praise of your grace,
In rhapsodic raptures my love when your voice greets.

The clouds burst in joy, love's light drizzle upon you,
To celebrate love, dear love, when two hearts meet.

Dusk blushes a scarlet, the moon eager to please,
Love, my love has charmed the sky and the ground beneath.

THE COLOUR OF ROSE SHARBAT

Not bitter, not sour,
not dark nor blue,
not loud not forced,
nor wrested out of you.

Not dull nor dry,
not limp nor pale,
but scented with the scent,
flowers exhale.

Soaked deep,
in scarlet ink,
smooth and flowing,
wanting nothing.

Fragrant red droplets,
that a bottle struts,
my love is the colour,
of rose Sharbat.

AGAIN AND AGAIN

It took a moment to fall in love,
With a blink of an eye I fell.

Knowing not how deep I went,
Blinded by Cupid's spell.

Sweet it was, sweet it is,
Love's unbridled reins.

And if all over I had to give my heart,
To you I'd give again.

Know not I of yesterday,
Its over and it's done.

Know not I of tomorrow,
Nor of the novel sun.

Know I of the moment now,
And love unbridled reigns.

And if I had to give my heart,
To you I'd give again.

HAIKU (LOVE)

Spinning web of love
In fine gossamer of thoughts
Delicate tangle

IF EYES ARE WINDOWS TO THE HEART AND SOUL

If eyes are windows,
to the heart and soul,
an inkling of what,
lies beneath the skin,

Then thank goodness,
for tresses that veil a face,
and hide midst waves,
what lies within.

If eyes are windows,
to the heart and soul,
then welcome shades,
dark, rose tinged,

A screen between the I,
and the world at day,
where none can see,
the core within.

If eyes are windows,
to the heart and soul,
a glimpse into fears, tears,
when a heart cries,

Then thank goodness,
it takes a moment,
to draw down lashes,
and close the eyes.

WILL YOU STILL LOVE ME

Today I'm beautiful,
And I have you on your knees,
But when my beauty wanes,
Will you still love me?

Today I'm young,
And passion has her say,
But will you hold me close,
When crimson love greys?

Today I'm alive,
Like a strong summer gale,
But will you care for me,
When I be frail?

Today I smile,
There's laughter in my eyes,
But will you be with me,
When my heart cries?

Will you love me, hold me,
In love's tender kiss,
When my hair turns white,
And my thoughts go a miss?

Will you love me, hug me,
Ever so tight,
Through my brightest morn'
In my darkest night?

JUST AS LOVE SHOULD

I loved you on a quiet day,
And I loved you on a stormy night,
I loved you through the fog and mist,
The sun's scourge burning bright.

I loved you like fire does,
Drops of water that keep alive,
Like wind that breathes on a leaf,
Like earth that cradles life.

I loved you on a rainbow,
When seven colours filled the sky,
On feathers of white hope,
As wings spanned across to fly.

I loved you when waves rested,
And when the river was serene,
When grass by it wilted yellow,
When waters turned shadowed green.

I loved you when the sun set,
And when the moon was veiled in clouds,
When the stars shrivelled and hid behind,
Despair's dark midnight shroud.

I loved you then and I love you now,
I loved you all I could,
And I love you through the beats of time,
Just as love should.

FALLING IN LOVE, STAYING IN LOVE

Falling in love is like being at sea,
Swept away, riding high on a heart's waves,
A rush, breathless, heady with scant control,
Consuming, a body and mind's incessant crave,
Incomplete without the other, a half of a larger whole.

Falling in love is walking in a world of dreams,
Eyes closed and content,
Part surreal, ethereal, a magical world,
Walking in fields of blossoms, nectar fragrant,
Music adrift where but lyrical melodies are heard.

Staying in love is being washed ashore,
When waters bring one back to where the land greets,
Knowing that waves will wash and toss once more,
On white, brown, black sands that hold unsteady feet.

Staying in love is walking awake in love's dreams,
Knowing when night is over and when begins the day,
Understanding that not all will be forever what seems,
That melodies may pause, winds may blow the fragrance away.

LOVING YOU IS EASY

Loving you is easy,
You know me like no one does,
You hear the whispers of my heart,
You hold the rhythm of my pulse.

Loving you is easy,
For you sense my every want,
Before words can shape desires,
Before desires come to haunt.

Loving you is easy,
With you I am just me,
I needn't veil my eyes,
Nor fear what you could see.

Loving you is easy,
For the tears you kiss away,
The words that calm my heart,
The smiles that make my day.

Loving you is easy,
For the love notes that you sing,
The beauty in your songs,
The magic that you bring.

Loving you is easy,
And it's all I seem to do,
When I look in your eyes,
I see all this love in you.

A SERENADE OF LOVE

Sweeter than the song of a nightingale,
Gentler than the whisper of a spring wind,
Quieter than the murmur of summer grass,
Softer than the symphony of hyacinths.

Hypnotic like the splash of blue seas,
Tinkling like a stream that flows,
Mesmerising like the cadence of rain,
Enchanting like the hush of snow.

Like the faint breath of a scarlet dawn,
The rustle of clouds on a turquoise high,
A duet of night and an ivory moon,
A Capella of stars in the sky.

A hymn, a chant, a choir of angels,
Singing on a rainbow of time,
Celestial is the serenade of love,
A tune and a note divine.

ALL FOR YOU

If only I could ease your pain,
If I could make you smile again,
If I could dream for you to see,
If I could charm reality.
If I could dry your quiet tears,
If I could scare your little fears,
If I could calm your every storm,
If I could wrap you, keep you warm,

If I could sear, scour and fly,
To the farthest corner of the sky,
If I could pluck those distant stars,
Of hopes that twinkle from a far,
Of sweet desires, old and new.
I'll bring them all right here for you . . .

A BIRD WITHOUT WINGS

Love me all you want to,
And let me cherished be,
But imprison not my soul, my thoughts,
For I long to soar free.

Let me breathe the way I want,
My own melodies sing,
I'll walk my walk, let me fly,
Bind not my feet or wings.

Though held by words, sacred ties,
Each one so distinct,
My own life, dreams, desires,
Cage not the way I think.

Enough space between two hearts,
Enough space between you and I,
Enough for sunrays to beam through,
Enough for gales to storm by.

Hold me close but never so tight,
That I can't spread my wings,
"How can a bird that's born for joy,
Sit in a cage and sing?"

(Inspired by Oscar Wilde)

A FRUITY POET POTPOURRI OF A VALENTINE VERSE

Vanilla vowels,
And creamy coloured consonants,
Naughty or nutty nouns,
Of almonds, apples, apricots,
Aphrodisiac adjectives,
And very berry adverbs,
Passion fruit phrases,
Pirouette like peaches in thought.

A pomegranate patter,
That pronounces a pronoun,
Or perhaps in veiled vines,
Velvet verbs purr,
Wondrously whipped,
Words of love,
Salacious sentences,
With strawberry stirred.

A mellowed muskmelon,
Of a metaphor,
A salubrious simile,
Sits like a sapote crown,
Amorous alliterative adventures,
With romance and raisins,
An ooh la la of orange oomph,
Onomatopoeic sounds.

An orchard of the alphabets,
In a fruity potpourri of speech,
A bearish pearish play,
Plum pun on words,
The language of love,
Written with love,
In this potpourri, bonhomie Valentine verse.

BEYOND TIME

It is said with fragrant lilac candles or with rich crimson roses,
in summer breeze perfumes.

It is sung in a soft melody, hummed in a symphony,
a haunting lover's tune.

It is penned in grandiose verse,
with a quill dipped in the red ink of the heart.

It is spelled in easy words,
hand printed a humble work of art.

It is sweetened with strawberry candies,
chocolate truffles arranged winsomely in a row.

It is toasted to with a bottle of chardonnay,
wrapped with scarlet ribbons as the ends kiss in a bow.

It is engraved in glimmering sterlings,
emeralds, moonstones in rich ruby sheen.

It is whispered breathless 'neath a star clad night,
under a galaxy of orbiting tinsel dreams.

But I need no floral bouquets no lilac candles,
no dark chocolates, no bottle of wine.

I need not even a rose, no paper confessions,
no treasures, no jewels divine.

I need no promises, no pledges,
no vows whispered you are mine,

My love is beyond this, beyond words,
beyond you and me,
beyond time.

THE HEART, THE BEAT, THE HEARTBEAT OF A COSMIC DANCE

Close your eyes,
fall in love,
let the full moon cast his spell,
falling, whirling,
in the circle of love,
deep down within it dwell.

Close your eyes,
kiss the stars,
let fireflies light your soul,
walk in fields,
of sterling silver,
where love pure magic holds.

Close your eyes,
touch the sun,
his rays a gold cocoon,
warm in the heat,
of loves fire,
stronger than the Sol in June.

Close your eyes,
feel the wind,
run against the skin,
the touch of love,
is like no other,
a caress from deep within.

Close your eyes,
inhale the blooms,
blossoms that love springs,
a scent that pours,
into the heart and mind,
every season the soul can sing.

Close your eyes,
fill the senses,
with the joy of love's glance,
'tis love that makes,
the world go round,
the heartbeat of cosmic dance.

IF I COULD WISH ON
A SHOOTING STAR

If I could wish on a shooting star,
I'd wish a heartfelt wish for you,
I'd wish for peace in your heart,
I'd wish for your happiness too.
If I chanced a genie in a bottle,
To him I'd but merely say,
To fly you on his silk carpet,
And rub your tears and fears away.
If I had a fairy godmother,
I'd ask her to make all well,
With a touch of her magic wand,
She'd cast a charm, a magic spell.

Now I have but these thoughts,
And earnest wishes I hope come true,
So I'll send them as little prayers,
To Him above just for you.

A WINDOW INTO INDIA

'NAMASTE'

A heart that salutes,
And greets,
Hands come together,
Palms touch,
As in prayer,
And fingers meet.

Head lowered,
A slight bow,
With respect due.
A gesture that reads,
The spirit in me honours,
The spirit in you.

A welcome to the young,
And old alike,
To a guest, a friend.
Anyone who might,
Walk your way,
A word when parting too.
When it's time to leave,
Turn and bid adieu.

A simple word,
Yet has much to say,
A word that wishes well and hopes,
For a beautiful and blessed day.

THE MAGIC OF JAIPUR, THE PINK CITY

The walls of Jaipur stand proud in pink,
Guarding the city in their rustic shade,
Softening the heat when Sol doesn't blink,
And the cold of bitterly dry winter days.
Ancient quilas and mahals with life still breathe,
More than inanimate concrete or mere bricks red,
A mosaic of tradition that heritage bequeaths,
Inscriptions of culture where history treads.

Hear the loud trumpet of elephants of yore,
The laughter of maharanis in palkis of gold,
The war cries of maharajas wielding glittering swords,
The words of a messenger from a jewelled scroll.
Portraits speak of liaisons and love,
Of courage in hearts and love's sighs,
Of wars waged, hands touched,
Yesterday lives through an artist's eyes.

In the desert trudge camels with men in white,
Thirsting their way in dhotis in summer dust storms,
Women in mirrored lahariya lehengas bright,
Weave cotton quilts to keep winter warm.
Folk songs fill a night beneath a canopy of stars,
Witness he was then and now the moon,
The music of the dholak, the sarangi and sitar,
Mingle with the whispers of sand dunes.

The streets shuffle busily with traders and craft,
With glimmering zari, gota, kinari and precious stones,
Blue pottery, marble figurines, painting and art,
Inspiration carved in artisans home.
Vivacious is Jaipur with her own heartbeat,
Her people, her streets throb with stories,
Not a moment quiet as past and present greet,
In the Pink City that revels in her glory.

BANGLES

Ornaments that delight, even in their simplicity subtly ornate,
Circles of rainbows in colours of life, flamboyant or hues subdued,
Creations in glass, a pistachio green, cotton candy pink, in myriad shades,
Clinking bangles in mulberry purple, majestic red or peacock blue.

In exclusive platinum or sparkling silver or a glimmering metallic gold,
Bridal jewels with gems, in exquisite work and beauty fair,
Precious symbols of love, an inheritance of priceless moulds,
Jingling bangles worn with pride and delicate care.

Colours and styles that often would a woman define,
An expression of marital ties, perhaps a mood or style she'd state,
Each bangle in perfect circular symmetry designed,
A reason beautiful enough to celebrate.

As wrists laden with bangles move to the beats of the 'dhol',
Bedecked in festive finery in tune with traditional occasions,
Songs of life sung, hymns to God or the notes of rustic folklore,
One can hear the music of bangles in life's little celebrations.

MEHR-UN-NISSA'S EYES

I wonder what they would be like, Mehr-un-nissa's enticing eyes,
The Emperor wrapped in their embrace . . . lost within, mesmerised.
Soft, sensual, sensuous . . . rich and sweet like summer wine,
Deep, dark, unfathomable seas, with dark kohl their depths defined.
Fiery green or passion's blue, a prism of colours, desire's lure,
Hazel, tawny with glints of gold, gentle, grey, brown, demure.
Alight with loves passionate glance, immortal loves soulful cries,
His heart, his world, his life . . . in Mehr-un-nissa immortalised.

A mirror to her soul, they'd be, Beauty herself in woman's guise,
With courage, wisdom, love endowed, the Empress of hearts in his eyes.

THE KASHMIRI RUG

It's a large hand knotted rug, made in Kashmir,
Reminiscent of less troubled days,
Of a heaven on earth, greens exquisite,
When peace smiled long enough and stayed.

It is multi dimensional with depth, breadth and length of yore,
Of songs sung as weavers wove in fine silken threads,
Ethnic motifs, intricate, delicate, a work of skilled artisans,
In shades of carrot pink, beige and a lyrical red.

It's been revered, from forefathers handed over,
Enduring, rooted, like the roots of the family tree,
From one generation handed to another,
And now with care handed to me.

It's lived in different cities, different countries,
Seen war, riots, peace in all her glory,
Seen disasters, natural or provoked by man,
And like it's fine weaves, it spins many a stories.

It recalls a massive earthquake in Quetta,
That demolished a home and belongings,
Efforts to salvage life, precious possessions,
A tale of loss and longing.

Of riots in Lahore, how an uncle was killed,
When violence won, love turned to hate.
Accidental victim of communal misunderstanding,
Dreams burnt to ashes in a quirk of fate.

It made its way to Delhi; in an independent India,
In a home in a historical city, quaint, old,
Packed tenderly by knotted, gnarled hands,
Faded a trifle but more precious than gold.

It graced many a homes across the seas,
An ambassador of a people, a country,
It's deep and warm shades,
Welcoming friends and families.

It witnessed the mayhem of ceremonies, the beauty of marital ties,
The celebrations, the festivities, all in a glance,
Of love, in a bride's kohl rimmed eyes.
The delicate blush of a summer romance.

And now it lays in stately elegance in the family room,
In quiet decor with nostalgia it blends,
A relic, a treasure of memoirs and memories,
Timeless, beautiful, though worn at the ends.

THE SNAKE CHARMER

The old wizened wrinkled snake charmer, with a red turban on his head,
A khaki bag across his shoulders, a dhoti wrapped around his legs.

He traces his ancestors path, makes his way through dusty lanes,
Calling out through his flute, hoping to cast his spell again.

A coiled cobra wrapped in a basket . . . his livelihood he carries around,
No doubts, no fear, with his snake the snake charmer walks the town.

Curious chatter, a fascinated child yearns to see the snake rise,
Dancing to the charmer's tune, a cobra or a viper mesmerised.

With the basket a distance away, the charmer sits crossed leg,
his tune to play,
The snake slowly uncoils serpentine, moving to the flute, it starts to sway.

A crowd gathers and like the snake,
it stands entranced with widened eyes,
The cobra dancing to the flute . . . with it's movement, hypnotised.

The snake raises it's head and lunges forward with a menacing hiss,
The snake charmer unperturbed plays his flute and gives death a miss.

Coins, notes, come the charmer's way . . . sighs, cheer, clear and loud,
A prayer in humble gratitude, the snake charmed, so the crowd.

THE PALMIST

On a quiet street, in a decrepit shop, sits the wise palmist,
Owl like visage, a network of zig zag lines on his forehead,
Deep creases that run across . . . like the lines on his palm,
His eyes sharp, alert, twinkle seeking hands that long to be read.

With his pair of well worn glasses, rimmed with gold at the ends,
An intricately engraved, copper toned magnifying glass . . .
his tool in his hands,
He clasps sweaty palms in his own, looking deep into them,
Glimpsing into the past, the present, the future, the web of life, the
master plan.

Bankers, students, lovers, politicians, call on him with queries,
Money, marriage, children, family, profession, disease,
Worried faces, tapping fingers, shuffling feet, hoping to sort
the business of life,
Searching for answers, a window into the future, clarity . . .
perhaps some peace.

People travel from far, there is a long queue outside his room,
Curiosity, a word of advice or hope, a blessing,
help in decisions to be made,
He'll sigh, he'll frown, raise his brows, crinkle his eyes, smile,
nod his head,
He is skilled, learned, intuitive, in fact, he is the best in his trade.

He glosses over the palm with his eyes, studies the mounts on fingers,
He examines the shape of a hand, the language of the fist.
He traces the fate line, he turns the hand from side to side,
Peers over the heart line, the head line, the life line reaching for the wrist.

An art, a science learned from his father, studied, perfected over the years,
He himself, however, is not sure where his life will turn and go.
For someone who has read many hands, he never reads his own,
Like his father, he takes life as it comes . . . he doesn't want to know.

THE INDIAN SILK SARI

Six yards of glistening threads,
Woven with hands for dreams to tread,
Draped in layers, that gently hold,
Caress of silk through soft folds.

Golden motifs, ethereal seem,
Woven with care, someone's dream,
Wrapped around in art's cocoon.
Wrapped deep in soft silken dunes.

Exotic hues with gold embraced,
Intricately woven, delicate grace,
Like tender petals, drapes allure,
Silk rich, sensual and pure.

Glimmering, shaded, passionate sheens,
Royal sheers to drape a queen,
Exquisite work, beauty preens,
In every sari, an artist seen.

THE NOTES OF THE BANSURI

The notes of the bansuri,
Lift and drift in the air,
Rising from the midst,
Of the sun baked,
Mud splattered home.
Lilting music, soft folk tunes,
Rustic allure to the ears.

A divine instrument,
That oscillates in flow,
In the temple and tempo of love.
Enchanting,
Imploring the beloved,
With a rasa lila of the heart.
Charming dancing maidens,
In rainbow glass bangles,
And silver anklets,
Yellow ghagras,
Mirrored Cholis,
In mesmeric tones.

Eyes closed,
A meditation in medley,
Fluted softly by a cowherd,
Tending cattle.
The latter enchanted,
Spell bound,
Follow the mellifluous notes home,
Finding their way.

The purest and simplest of sounds,
That resonates,
In every cell of the being,
Inspiring, uplifting,
Soothing, calming,
A balm to existence,
Mere breath flowing,
Through bamboo,
In an artist's hand,
Turns celestial.

RANGOLI, A FOLK ART

The art of creating colourful and appealing designs on the floor,
Rangoli, made from petals, vermillion, flour, paints or powdered rice.
Women decorating a courtyard, an entrance in life's casts,
In geometric patterns, motifs, simple aesthetics pleasing to the eyes.

A part of folk art, folklore, among the many stories that go,
The son of a priest was from death revived,
As Brahma with mercy breathed into his image,
And through a painted canvas on the floor, bestowed him with life.

Auguring good luck, a symbol of happiness, gracious hospitality,
As with the break of morning, a new day starts,
With paints, powder or petals, that draw figurines, peacocks,
Flowers, candles, . . . a woman's very own everyday art.

On the threshold of a house like a bridge that binds,
Connecting what's out with hearts within,
A glimpse into the culture of a home,
And all the love that a hearth brings.

Pink, green, blue, red or white . . . hues wet and dry,
Shades celebrate the tones that life imbibes,
And as the colours wash, blow, wither and disappear,
A subtle reminder of the impermanence of life.

TWO HEARTS BEATING AS ONE

Every morn, in trepidation, she would wait,
    Her heart alive in love's murmurs,
    Her eyes gleaming in anticipation,
    To steal a glimpse of the Emperor.

She would wait to catch his silhouette,
Or perhaps, hear the footfall of his feet,
    Lingering by the jharoka,
For a moment their eyes would meet.

She was a courtesan, no princess royal,
He was the monarch, the sun, regality,
Two different worlds, different legacies,
A love, a union that could never be.

Yet when she'd sing her song,
Her love filled notes, her melody,
In the magic of her lilting voice,
She knew his heart would captive be,

Midst the sound of her bangles,
The gentle rhythm of her feet,
The steady taal of the tabla,
She'd hear his quiet heart beat.

For those brief sweet moments,
Unmeasured precious bliss,
Two hearts would beat as one.
For those sweet moments,
He was hers and she was his.

THE UMBRELLA

It is a canopy, made of cloth that blocks rain out,
In coloured stripes of red, green, yellow and a mellow blue.
Old, faded, a tottering handle, but functional, still a cover,
She holds it close to herself, a precious possession.
She knows when the rains come, the deluge, the torrent,
It was all she would have as shelter.
It would rain for hours, unendingly . . . incessantly . . . persistently . . . .
Beating on the asphalt roads, pounding, thundering, deafening, like the
hooves of a hundred horses.
On roof tops, on windows, on the traffic, blinding it, drowning it.
Whiplashes of rain.
And her hair would drip, her clothes wet, clinging, damp for hours.
When the wind would pick up at night, it would chill her.
Her bones would become stiffer, it would be hard for her to take those
few steps.
She shivers just at the thought of it.
She could never know the joy of soaking in the rain.
She does not want to. She cannot afford to. She cannot bear the thought
of raindrops on her face.
She cringes looking at the sky, a darkening expanse.
She cringes looking at herself. Her bedraggled rags.
The footpath, her makeshift home. A small bundle, her belongings.
The walking stick; her support.
If fortunate, she might find space beneath a parapet.
She holds the umbrella closer. Clutches it tighter.
It is the same umbrella that has screened her from the rays of the sun.
Over the years;
The intensity of its rays, the intensity of its heat, the intensity of summer.

To the man who drives by in his car, as he glances at her indifferently,
through his gold rimmed glasses . . . over the newspaper . . . it is just
that . . .
an umbrella.

To her, it is shelter. Her roof. Her home.

THE MISTRESS OF SPICES

Step into to her world, a world where she lives,
Of colours a plenty and flavours many,
A flick of a hand, in measures she gives,
Spices that tantalise, worth every penny.
Red chillies an ounce, turmeric a pound,
Spices scarlet, yellow, in hues exotic,
Peppercorns, cardamoms, whole or ground,
Brown bay leaves, cinnamon, aromatic.
Wonders for the body that soothe and heal,
Nurturing from nature, a stoic promise,
From the choicest gardens, as senses reel,
Fragrance of flavours in sensual bliss.

Within her world, another world entices,
Her voice in sweet whispers has tales to tell,
Magic in dark eyes, the mistress of spices,
With a flick of her hand, she'll cast a spell.

(inspired by the title of the book by Chitra Divakaruni)

BASANT PANCHMI

Dressed in a warm vivacious yellow,
Comes sweet February and reigns,
Winter rests, spring like a nascent sun,
Rises fiery soft in golden flames.

Amber sparkles on a bed of fields,
As crops glisten in Aurelia's rays,
Gentle winds run through mustard flowers,
A sea of florals ripple with copper waves.

In ghagras, women dance with joy,
The sound of dhol resonates in the air,
Songs of harvest as arms move,
Signs of spring bloom everywhere.

The land throbs with life in pastels,
The cerulean sky now pulsating bright,
Carried by a tingling breeze,
On hearts soar a thousand kites.

Of Kesar is the vasant season,
Halwa sprinkled with fragrant saffron,
Wrap ye all in sunshine now,
On the horizon see a summer sun.

Beaming sunflowers and marigolds,
Burst open with robust flair,
In offering to the goddess of nature and art,
A bouquet of hymns in a prayer.

THE ROAD AFTER INDEPENDENCE

On the same road lies the Shiva temple, the church,
The mosque, the gurudwara where thousands pray,
The vendor who sells bhel, vada pao,
The upscale restaurant that dishes out gourmet kebabs,
Malabar paranthas, poriyal served on silver trays.

Everyday thousands brush against each other,
The turban or sherwani clad men . . . shoulders straight and proud,
Women behind veils, in silk zari saris, kalaamkari prints,
Kajaal darkened eyes in vivacious batik,
Each one their own yet of the crowd.

Differences transcend borders and homes,
Eid Mubarak as Hindus and Muslims embrace,
Firecrackers burst through religions and status,
Christmas where love is gifted,
And the colors of Holi brighten every face.

It is here the flower girl sits stringing garlands,
A delicate trail of jasmine to grace a maiden's hair,
And its here the old widow eats her frugal meal,
Of chapatis and daal,
With gratitude and a prayer.

The bullock cart is as much a part of this road,
As are those cows and chauffeur driven cars,
The labourers, the beggars, the lawyers, the jewelers,
The page 3 designer boutiques,
That ordinary but vibrant roadside bazaar.

On the same road, we meet, from 'Kashmir to Kanyakumari',
Despite scattered hopes on a broken road, in our hearts a distinct gleam,
For one day we'll make it together,
On this road . . . . to an India, a country of our dreams.

FOR THE INDIAN WOMEN

IN AN ANGEL'S SMILE

Little footsteps, a smile with braces, arms of love that embrace,
Fists that pound a brother down, rose cheeks on an impish face.

Tangled hair in mystic knots, hesitant eyes that shy away,
Youth blossoms with hope in eyes when dreams come to stay.

Warmth in a heart that blushes red, shoulders wrapped in curls,
Strength builds on aspirations, grit to face the world.

A tender bud that yearns to grow, some sunshine and some air,
Heavens rains will nurture her in a garden of tender care.

Oh let her grow, let her feel the beauty from spring to winter,
The moon and dew will dance together on her nimble fingers.

See her script her story; let her paint the skies,
Let the world build itself in an angel's smile.

CHILD BRIDE, NOT YET A WOMAN

She was asked to look coy, demure.
She was asked to deploy tactics to lure.
She was asked to charm with grace,
Disarm, amaze.
She was asked to whisper soft; in murmurs talk.
Like a paradigm of beauty, an artist's rendition.
On duty of empty, makeshift tradition.
She was asked to walk slow, head bent,
Eyes low. Shy and smile content.

While . . . while she longed to run free,
In bewilderment was she.
The toe rings were pinching,
Hunger was inching.
Like a bejewelled chandelier
All sparkling fare.
Trapped and wrapped.
She had smiled and smiled,
Till it riled. So fake, her jaws ached.
Her kohl rich eyes sighed.
Longing for simple pleasures.
Treasures.
Bare feet with dirt,
A bellowing wind blown skirt.

No clanking glass bangles,
Hair undone, tousled,
Untamed, entangled.
Flowers tickling, rain trickling,
Rolling on hills, till laughter spilled.
She yearned to run away, hide,
From peering faces, this child bride.
From inquisitive noses, exploring looks,
Delve into the comfort of her books.
Her heart spoke, her voice choked.
Quiet words.Unsaid, unheard.
She yearned for childhood, lost,
Unbridled youth, dreams tossed,
Shackled, bound on all sides,
Not yet a woman, this child bride.

DEPRAVITY

A baby girl barely born,
Perhaps unwanted or unplanned,
Confronts death in her first cry,
Smothered by familiar hands.

A girl child barely two lies battered,
With bite marks, broken bones abused,
A childhood marred, memories blurred,
A life fragmented, forever bruised.

A young girl is stolen from her hearth,
As consuming lust has his way,
In a moment innocence lost,
As she dies a death every day.

A woman, a wife, a mother,
Live in fear, a shadowed haze,
Sacredness of ties is scarred,
In fits of drunken nauseous rage.

Worshipped, of course, is a woman,
As a deity . . . or so it seems,
While one hand folds in devout prayers,
The other stifles her quiet screams.

Oh yes, bow, chant, pray,
Kneel with devotion on your knees,
And once done with incense sticks,
Treat her just the way you please.

Perhaps a couple of hands will help,
Perhaps some heads will hang in shame,
But broken women are just numbers,
Listless figures without names.

Blame her for ills done to her,
Provocation, enticement as you deem fit,
For there is no end to depravity,
In a society of hypocrites.

THE WORLD, I HOLD

Born of a tired womb
Held by hands, work weary
Midst echoes of hunger and thirst
Beneath the shadow of an indifferent heart hardened with poverty
Fed from a near empty bowl, shouldering an empty satchel
On coarse grains of sands
I STAND

Trudging roads, retrieving and holding snippets of snatched dreams
Beneath the fiery pounding sun that torches the skin
A tattered ragged book in hand
In the other, crude coloured plastic that holds water
Endless days of drudgery and cries
I RISE

With empty hands I write
Trudge relentlessly on the path of destiny
Fixing broken roads, mending dreams
My life in my hand
Days of toil and a pen at night
I SURPRISE

To those that put me back
To those that shove, to those who scorn
To those who don't let live
I STILL GIVE

My head held high, I walk, I work
I feed, I nurture, I nurse, I teach, I love
Within my heart, within its folds
The world I HOLD

AND WHO ARE YOU TO JUDGE ME?

Have you walked my path
And drudged my miles
Have you felt my pain
Or held my heart
Have you heard my voice
Sung my songs
Have you seen me fight
For my right, my wrong

Who are you to judge me?

Have you seen my morning
Or darkness in dusk
Have you braced my summer
The bite of winter
Have you braved my storms
Or the waves that wreck
My hands, my mind
My soul in shreds

Who are you to judge me?

You who stand back and

Chide

Deride

Decide

That I am weak
And you are strong
Your way is right
Mine is wrong

Who are you to judge me??

IN THE ARENA

I dropped the veil that conceals me,
the handcuffed thoughts that bind,
the chains that hold me tight,
the shackles that still my flight.

Beyond four brick confining walls,
beyond beaded curtains that fall,
beyond edicts that restrictions brace,
I crossed and found my place.

I am in orchards, vineyards and fields,
in plantations and towers of steel,
in board rooms made with teak and awe,
in campuses and courts of law.

Midst the flowers and candles,
cradles, ladles, pens, desk and tea,
I can raise a torpedo of troops,
I can make a home, raise a baby.

I marched across the wide divide,
I struggled and dared and tried,
In between the cries and whys,
I found my place with pride.

REFLECTIONS ON LIFE DARKNESS AND LIGHT

ALL THAT MATTERS

A PRAYER.
HE WILL SEE YOU THROUGH

I hope your day is beautiful,
With sunshine, bright and fair,
Embraced by those who love you,
Who hold you close and care.

I hope your day is warm,
With the blanket of His love,
That envelops the world around,
From realms below to those above.

I hope your day is calm,
And as peaceful as can be,
He'll stand by those who need him,
With them, with you and me.

I hope your day brings joy,
Reprieve from grief and pain,
So tomorrow you may love,
Smile and laugh again.

I hope your day is a Blessing,
Know He walks every step with you,
For if He has brought you thus,
I know He will see you through.

WOULD YOU KNOW THE COLOUR OF MUSIC

Would you know the colour of music?
White, black or grey,
Would you know the melodies that air?
What colours are they?

Would you know the notes that flow?
The hues that come your way,
Are they a rainbow of colours,
As many tunes as they play?

A part of a larger symphony,
Man is music from His soul,
Music from His heart,
Music that should extol.

Hearts alive with rhythmic beats,
Drum akin beneath the skins,
Not just where the rainbow ends,
But where it all begins.

HAIKU (FRIENDSHIP)

Friendship is a fort,
Friend a gallant warrior,
Armed in love's defense.

CAPRICE

Like a stream that meanders,
Cantering music sweet,
Caprice treads whimsical,
Lightly on her feet.

Like the wind that doesn't know,
Where to gently breeze,
Caprice breathes here, then there,
. . . the air touched 'n teased.

Like the midnight stars that twinkle
Through the darkness peer,
Caprice in a wink,
Appears to disappear.

Like the morning sunlight,
That hides, then lights up hills,
Caprice scampers up and down,
Never a moment still.

Like waves and ocean tides,
That ebb, rise and flow,
Caprice heaves night and day . . .
Between her joys and woes.

Like raindrops and the rainbow,
That hold the other's hand,
Caprice sighs and smiles,
In but a single glance.

I wonder . . . if you sense her,
Her murmurs, feel her warm breath.
Caprice . . . right behind you.
Though you haven't seen her yet.

THROUGH STRUGGLE
THROUGH THE STARS

On days it rains a thunderstorm,
It pours for hours and hours,
It rains on a struggling heart and soul,
It rains a torrid shower.

But once the clouds of rain are done,
The travail of tears is dry,
Once the battling storm has raged,
A rainbow brightens up the sky.

On the rainbow that lights the realms,
If I could just ascend,
Soaking, living it's myriad colours,
Riding on its bend.

High astride on the arc of hope,
Going up, away and far,
Tempests waged within and out,
Through struggle to the stars.

'LOVE ME WHEN I LEAST DESERVE IT'

There are times I know not who I be,
A stranger, unreasonable, I become,
Little sense in the world around I see,
'Tween love and hate, on a pendulum.

There are times I turn away from you,
Question your love, your wise decree,
Eyes wide shut to whatever you do,
Believing you too have forsaken me.

There are times I doubt, if at all you exist,
My heart, to darkness, a welcome home.
Your presence denied, you I resist,
Hope burns in doubt's infernal dome.

Love me when I least deserve; when to despair, a host,
Hold me God, for it is then . . . that I need your love the most.

THE PURSUIT OF HAPPINESS

In the pursuit of happiness I walked the roads,
I stopped at milestones, leaned on posts.
I saw a flock of birds in flight,
Rings of gold, an orb so bright.
I looked around at mountain walls,
The raging sea, white frothy falls.
I looked up at the sky serene,
The valley lush a summer green.
Banyan trees with leaves bedecked,
Gulmohars lined with blossoms red.

Faces walked engrossed in streets,
A touch, a nod when eyes would meet,
Hunger, anguish, weary eyes,
Terror, sorrow, shock, surprise,
I saw the tears of loss and grief,
Faith, resilience, resolve, belief.
I heard the laughter of a child,
I saw the magic of a smile.
A hug, a kiss, a warm caress,
A helping hand that love expressed,
I felt the cord of love that binds,
Hearts across the world and time.

I found happiness in little things,
In nature that surprises springs,
His art, the colours that I saw,
That left me breathless, full of awe,
Happiness in that special touch,
In smiles, laughter, that gentle brush.
In kind words that wonders do,
In love that breathes life anew.
In all things that I could see,
I knew happiness begins with me,
Within me what I see or do,
The trail of thoughts I send to you.
And happiness is what I found,
When happiness was spread around.

FRAGILE STILL

She seems strong, so she speaks,
She seems alive, with life complete.
She shrugs a shoulder, couldn't care,
Love is war, a life's dare,
She has loved and seen it go,
Love wilt in the midst of snow . . .
But say goodbye, gently, if you will,
Her heart is warm, fragile still.

She has laughed, she has smiled,
Dreamed enchantment, on an isle.
She has risen, heights soared,
She has seen closed doors.
She has fallen, again, to stand,
Dreamed a dream in never land . . .
But tread softly, on her, if you will,
Her dreams are young, fragile still.

She has seen, loss and pain,
Prayers lost, hopes slain.
Her heart in hands, she has wept,
Tired and weary, troubled, slept.
Transience is eternal, well she knows,
But her heart stronger, never grows . . .
Break her gently, if you will.
She is tender and fragile still.

US

Though a clock should know precision,
Should know when to chime,
But it is a creation,
That too varies in time.

Human consciousness isn't linear,
Nor thoughts vertically aligned,
Emotions cannot be called,
To assemble in straight lines.

What can be said of man,
Impossible to define,
Can he be compartmentalised,
Into channels, clear and fine?

His present, past and future,
His heart and his mind,
Mould him invariably,
But each, a special design.

No whorls of fingers are similar,
Nor snowflakes that gently fall,
Nor footsteps one leaves behind,
Or inner voices, that call.

Perspectives are divergent,
Thoughts richly diverse,
Emotional intricacies varied,
Like souls that emerge.

Yet on the same enriching journey,
On a day we are born,
And back to where we should be,
In a day we are gone.

THE EGOISTICAL EGOTIST

"I me myself" and nothing beyond,
Singing your own melody,
Strumming your own song,
Stringing tunes of self adulation,
Humming along,
A medley of your glorification,
Where you for you belong.

You blow your own trumpet
Loud and clear,
Assuming other than that,
Nothing, no one will hear.
Drowning other songs that surround you,
To you, no music, but yours is true.

The vocalist, the drummer, the guitarist rolled in one,
The only one man orchestra and after you're done,
With expectant authority, you wait for applause,
Unwilling to accept or admit any flaws.

What you compose, you call symphony,
What I hear, I call cacophony.
Listen to your music with my ears,
You'll be surprised at what you hear.

Its such a pity that you are so off-key,
A pity that you can't hear or see.

MOST GRACIOUS

Beauty, most gracious, seems to be,
When bathed in quiet humility,
But clad with obsession, most vain,
Her face forever is marked 'n stained.

Wealth, richest appears to be,
When wrapped in kind generosity,
Wealth, may further, wealth impart,
For truly rich, is a generous heart.

Love, most rare, is when you'd see,
Caring and selfless magnanimity.
With love the world embraced be,
A hug wide enough for humanity.

Knowledge, most wise, appears to be,
When it shares humbly, in dignity,
Learning writ with pedantic arrogance,
Is no learning but a fool's ignorance.

Art, most special would appear to be,
When coloured with God's own decree,
Of life, beauty, wisdom, a rich wreathe . . .
That nurtures and happiness bequeaths.

Life, complete, would seem to be,
With health, bliss and serenity,
Enriched by friends and family . . .
And understanding of one's mortality.

DANCE AWAY

Loosen your collar,
Untie your tie.
Remove the worrying furrow,
From between your eyes.

Roll up your sleeves,
Kick off your shoes,
A pair of flip flops,
. . . Those old ones will do.

No thought, no man,
No treasure, no dime,
That brings you down,
Is worth any time.

There. That's better . . . .
Now that you've found you,
Sing your heart out,
And dance away the blues.

ASK NOT FOR THAT

I would give away beauty,
for beauty fleeting is.
Now to behold on the morrow amiss.
I would give away youth,
passion possessed.
Fire from within,
the burning, the quest,
I would give away wealth,
for no riches I care.
Happiness nought in shards of solitaire.
I'd give away my heart,
though never it was mine.
In me, perhaps,
for a moment in time.

But ask not for that,
that I hold close.
The sweetest of joys,
that forever grows.
Though it may never be,
what all it seems,
Ask not of me,
to give away my dream.

THE STARLET. THE DIVA. THE MUSE

Full of worshiped whisperings,
Hearts would heave and sigh,
Tinsel tinged stardust,
Sprinkled in her eyes,
Her glance a shining ebony,
An enticing silken gleam,
Her lips a rosy crescent,
Her hair a raven sheen.

A song and she the lyrics,
A poem and she the muse,
A painting and she the diva,
Painted in a palette of hues.
Her eyes would hold her lovers,
She a diva of fire,
Rolled in satin sheets,
In the arms of desire.

On stage, she a performance,
Her act of blood and sweat,
Her voice a harp, sheer music,
Oh, she'd take away your breath.
Dark lashes would set a quiver,
Pulses throbbing fast,
The spell of beauty and glitter,
Would it ever last?

Fortune is a fickle friend,
And fickle is fleeting fame,
A star rises then to dust,
Then alas, but a name.
Her voice is now subdued,
The sparkle of tinsel dulled,
Her eyes seek her former glory,
In the silence and lull.
Each star a dazzling shooting star,
Then a trail of whispers heard,
Dimmed in fading spotlight,
'Tis the way of the world.

THE SOCIAL BUTTERFLY

Like a puppet on a string,
She'll dance. She'll sing.
With grace and charm,
Fly her pretty wings.

She'll laugh for a while,
Beam a smile.

And they?

They'll all stop at this.
They'll tell her,
How lovely her smile is.

But stop a little longer,
If you dare,
Look her in her eyes
And tell her;
Do you really see a smile there?

ON JEALOUSY

What is it I see in your eyes,
I hear it when you call,
It follows me wherever I go,
It follows me in my footfalls.

What is it I have,
And you feel you don't,
Nothing at all, if I may say.
Open your eyes but you won't.

You're like me, everyone else,
Blessed by Him too,
Created by the same hands aren't we.
So what is it that bothers you?

Waste a lifetime hating me,
Your thoughts will tear you asunder,
Blame yourself and not me,
If you believe I steal your thunder.

A moment to spare then look within,
There is all of you to celebrate,
In a mind free from jealous hate,
Love and beauty reverberate.

THERE'S ALWAYS TOMORROW?

Isn't there always tomorrow?
Another day standing tall?
Of course, there would be tomorrow,
And on that morrow I would call.

Perhaps we'd meet for lunch,
Go shopping . . . linger over tea,
Spend a noon together, tomorrow,
Like we used to, you and me.

But then, somehow, I never called,
And that tomorrow never came,
One day faded into another,
Each day was just the same.

I did never get to know,
What you were going through.
I was just a call away,
But there was always much to do.

Days turned in to months,
I let time lapse and fly,
And I was far . . . far too late,
To even say goodbye.

I always thought there's tomorrow,
The promise of another day,
But I forgot time never ceases,
And life may never stay.

REALITY

I built a ceiling over my head,
A fortress around me,
I bubble wrapped my heart tight,
So reality couldn't confound me.
On wings of fantasy I soared high,
I delved into the deep sea,
I buried myself in a burrow,
And I let reality be.
But how long can I run,
And not confront what'll be,
How long before I can look at it
And not let it overwhelm me?
For all hideouts and escapades,
For a refusal to pause and see,
How long before I can hide no more,
How long before it finds me?

HAIKU
(THE NEW YEAR'S SUNRISE)

Orange pink delight,
Fires light expectant skies,
A golden sunrise.

Sunrays in a line,
Beaming sunlit warm sunshine,
A blessing divine.

New hopes born today,
New Year's promises will stay,
Hope will find a way.

ONE DAY AT A TIME

Now and then when we walk,
Life lays ahead of us,
Stumbling blocks.

And we trip, skip, we stall,
We lose our grip,
We fall.

But we carry on our own way,
However we can,
(I pray).

We lean, rest and hope,
Steady, unsteady,
Cope.

Eyes looking down up, blurred,
But looking ahead,
And forward.

Just one step at a time,
And then some,
Taking on life . . . each day,
As it comes.

A FACADE

Hair brushed perfect,
Slick, in vogue and style,
A fixed plastic smile,
That never reaches the eye.

The elite designer tie,
Pure silk that cotton mocks,
Is smooth and soft,
Not different from suave talk.

The crisp white shirt,
Impeccably starched,
Worn with panache,
Conceals a stiffer heart.

Trousers custom made,
Smart status state,
Walk with arrogance,
In conceited gait.

Shoes polished shine,
Clicking smart heels,
Nothing else but dark,
All a leather feel.

To the world he appears to be,
Well groomed, an inspiring man,
But they can't see him,
Like I can.

I watch him, I know him,
For right there I am,
A parade of finesse,
A facade, a sham.

And though he dresses,
With immaculate care,
His insides are unkempt,
His soul threadbare.

THE CLOWN

A palette of paint to paint his face,
Clothes full of hues bright,
A round red nose that bobs like a ball,
He is ready with a smile.

Comic antics that delight folks,
He rides, slides, cartwheels and falls,
Slips on banana peels, juggles fruit,
Tickled faces all.

When night comes, off comes the paint,
The nose, the wig, the clothes bright,
In dwindling darkness he rests himself,
Now his face he hides.

A jester, he jested, he cheered,
A camouflage in art,
But to himself, alone and quiet,
He rests his aching heart.

An act extraordinaire,
How he does beguile,
But to himself, now alone,
Who'll make the jester smile?

UNFATHOMABLE EYES

She stood quietly in a corner,
In worn out weathered rags,
Apart, aloof, alone,
With a decrepit, empty bag.

Her eyes seemed vacant,
Far in the distance she gazed,
Her eyes looked clouded,
Disenchanted and dazed.

I tried to read her mind,
I wondered what she thought,
Such unfathomable eyes,
In such emptiness caught.

A child walked to her,
Whispered in her ear,
He gently led her away.
As if resting a fear.

Then I knew it . . . I should have known,
But why couldn't I see?
Her eyes had no light of their own,
But what happened to me?

Often we arrive at conclusions,
Prejudiced or predisposed,
Clouded is our vision,
Our minds are often closed.

There is much more beyond,
Than what meets the eye,
Reality may be obscure,
HIdden, sheathed and shy.

CREATING TOMORROW

Ten tiny little fingers, ten tiny little toes,
Little ears agog,
A stubby little nose.

Tiny alert eyes that devotedly follow,
Little bundles of love,
Creating tomorrow.

An innocent smile, a curious grin,
A dimpled cheek,
A cleft on the chin,

Worms, mud, paper, paraphernalia swallowed,
Tumbling toddlers,
The world's tomorrow.

On Pegasus, unicorns, or dragons that fly,
A million queries,
How and why.

Thoughts ingenious or from a friend borrowed,
Children on a voyage,
Creating tomorrow.

Adolescent hopes with dreams yet real,
Rebellion within,
With crusading ideals.

Challenging a world, farcical, hollow,
Explosive teens,
Paving tomorrow.

Kindling their minds, lighting a spark,
Illuminating their way,
in the darkest of dark.

Teaching them right, guiding their way.
Creating tomorrow,
Starting today.

WHERE DOES BEAUTY LIVE?

For some, here's where beauty resides,
In a face or curve that sways with pride,
In full lips or alabaster skin,
In looks that charm and locks that win.

And for some, in crisp paper she stays,
And flaunts herself every day,
In labels and class attires,
In bought style, in pursuits, desire.

Some can vouch she's found in gold,
In rubies and stones of old,
In rings that are rich with appeal,
Oh, here . . . this is beauty. Feel.

Some rush to exotic places,
For there the moon truly amazes,
The sun sets with a special hue,
Unparalleled are the hills in view.

But we all know where beauty dwells,
Not long in lips that cast a spell,
Not on brows where she resides,
But in a heart true, deep inside.

Not found she is in terrains rare,
But outside she waits, her soul bare,
Behold and she's in your eyes,
In the ordinary, undisguised.

And yet how we still flounder and stray,
When beauty comes and walks our way,
Fools, we may never learn,
How oft do we beauty spurn?

SHANGRI LA

I long to go to Shangri La, I've been there once before,
If I could go to Shangri La, it'd be yesterday once more.

I sailed the splendid seven seas and reached the city's shores,
On a mermaid's moon kissed back, above the ocean floor.

We rode on silver waves so large, through many a coral reefs,
Through lost treasures, mounds of trinkets, buried so ever deep.

My eyes marveled wide with wonder, for I was but a child,
To reach the rare utopian land, the land of a thousand smiles.

Disease was rare, death was gentle, the old man was a sage,
Where those not so young were revered, 'twas the golden age.

Where children ran without worry, beyond a mother's sight,
Where every woman was a lady, every man was crowned a knight.

The earth, the moon, the sun, the stars . . . in benevolence bestowed,
Nature and man were in harmony, their auras gently glowed.

A mystic light hung in air, perceptible, benign,
Where everything I touched was pure, blessed and divine.

In wonder I saw this glorious land, robed in innocence,
I reveled in marvels of this world, cloaked in ignorance.

I left the shores of Shangri La, I had to travel wide,
Carrying memories of this land, though I was a naive child.

I yearn to see this world once more, I have seen it long before,
Would it have withstood the ravages of time . . .
my splendid world of yore?

WHAT IF I WEREN'T ME

I wonder what it would be like to be,
Someone else other than me,
Different eyes, a different nose,
A different face, I suppose.
A different smile, not so wide,
A little dimple on the side.
These unruly locks that I keep,
The tousled look, as if up from sleep.
And though I look a trifle insane
Would it change with a tidy mane?

What if my heart were not the same?
Cold and dark without a flame?
Would I still brood, with tears cry?
Every time I said goodbye?
What if my mind were obsessed?
With materialism possessed?
Would my soul with my mind abide
Or would it from my depths hide?

As I ruminate, there is no end,
But I know that God truly meant,
Me to be just me,
The way I have been sent.

IN A BUBBLE

I live in a bubble, I float in the air,
Cocooned, wrapped,
Without a care.

My world is gold, my world is pink,
Within it I sleep,
Within it blink.

Through the valley, over the stream,
Winds carry me,
In a dream.

I bounce off hills, I touch a tree,
An auburn leaf,
Flies by me.

A thin wall separates us though,
The grey world,
Still I know.

The bubble will burst, no doubt,
When it does,
I'll step out.

Till then, on clouds of white,
I'll dance within,
With delight.

A HELPING HAND

Words once uttered cannot be retracted,
Harsh words spoken sting for long,
'Tis difficult to forget what once was said,
Difficult to right such a wrong.

Words uttered in haste or rage,
In impatience, sardonic tones that mock,
Tear apart relationships,
Create walls and painful stumbling blocks.

But words spoken carefully,
Firm, yet gentle, though chiding one,
Work quietly, in wondrous ways,
Correcting wrongs that have been done.

Words may hurt, words may heal,
Words may well just break a man,
But words spoken with care and thought,
May well become a helping hand.

ON FORGIVENESS

Forgiveness is a blessing,
For him who gives,
And for him who receives.
The key to inner healing,
Unlocked and unleashed.
A stepping-stone to tranquility,
A soul released.
Blessed by divinity,
The doorway to peace.

I COLOURED MY WORLD

I coloured my world today.
My hands smeared in pastels,
Canary yellows,
Ripe peaches and cardinal ochres,
Pink from a flamingo sunrise,
A passionate cerise.
Splashed,
An array of feisty blues,
A flamboyant turquoise,
A topaz tango,
A twinkling periwinkle.
Streaked it with gold,
Contoured lilac smudges,
Lavender tipped edges,
In custard pineapple floats.
Splattered emeralds, toned pistachio,
Fern greens with swift finger strokes,
Tempered it with,
Muddy crusty earthy browns,
Rock coloured sandy mounds,
Reined in royal purple,
The sensual blaze of a flaming sunset,
The dark indigo of a gloaming sky,
Agate drops a few,
A silver sliver of a crescent new.

I coloured my world,
With my eyes,
My fingers, hands,
My hues,
Just the way I wanted to.

LIFE IS, LIFE ISN'T

Life is a few moments,
Today here, tomorrow not,
Far too fleeting to harbour anger,
Sail on grudges,
In heartburn caught.

Life isn't always a bed of flowers,
It's prickly thorns, sallow weeds,
But the beauty of those flowers,
Is a blessing,
Precious wreathe.

Life isn't always golden sunshine,
Its intermittent clouds with spells of rain,
Yet showers bring sweet reprieve,
And make the world,
Whole again.

Life isn't black and white,
It's many shades, red to grey,
A different colour colours us,
Fills us up,
Every day.

Life isn't a straight road,
It bends and twists day and night,
Turns so intricate,
What may seem wrong,
Might be right.

Life is to be cherished,
To work, play, laugh, love and give,
Hold those special close to you,
Look ahead,
Each moment live.

OF A SMILE AND A PRAYER

What kind of smile will you wear today?

The angry one that defiantly says,
No matter what hurdles, no matter how blue,
I'll smile. I'll laugh my way through.

Or the smile that is damp, so artfully feigned,
A quiver, you do all you can,
To hide the pain.

Then there's the smile that is forced, that never reaches the eye,
That screams and pretends,
There is a better I.

Perhaps the one that is ruthless, with a cruel glint,
Like the heartless villains,
All menace tinged.

Maybe like the smile of a pirate, with gold or dark teeth,
Ending in laughter,
Stolen treasures at his feet.

Or the smile that baffles, in coloured chemistry,
Like Mona Lisa's,
Obfuscates with mystery.

Not these . . . I hope.

I hope your smile is true, even though crooked or bent,
And means what it says,
"I'm fine and content".

Toothy or even perhaps toothless,
But one that radiates,
Peace and happiness.

Maybe simple yet wide, bewitching and calm,
That suns the world,
Acts like a charm.

Like a child's with a dimpled cheek,
Popping in and out with joy . . .
. . . As he giggles and speaks.

A true smile,
Is a blessing, a work of art,
And so beautiful when,
It comes from the heart.

Today, I hope and with all my heart pray,
That you have a reason,
To smile,
A real smile everyday.

NO. NOT TODAY

No shadows of yesterday,
Will cloud now,
No clouds of tomorrow,
Shadow today,
The sky may be bright or dark,
I'll see what I see,
Without grey.

Memories of the past,
Won't haunt,
What future brings,
I cannot see,
But in now will I linger,
For today,
Yesterday and tomorrow,
Will have to be.

Hands of time pull and tug,
Creating furrows,
In the brow,
But today I will not,
Be held ransom,
For I must make the most,
Of now.

Smooth or cobbled,
Petals or pebbles,
All shall come my way,
But why should I let,
A cobweb of a thought,
Steal my day,
Today.

WITHIN I AM

Hair be raven, golden, russet,
And eyes be ebony, green or blue,
Lips be red dipped in wine,
Skin almond or a rosy hue.

Hands be frail, creased with lines,
Soles worn with cracked feet,
Spine bent a storm-wrecked tree,
But a voice melodic sweet.

Waves wash in virgin waters,
Forests make a leafy throne,
Petals make a crown of blossoms,
Mountains mould a stone.

In the eyes dance reflections,
A mirror of what I can see,
You say I am not a stranger,
Then pray tell me who I be.

One by one, I drop a layer,
And still I be a whole,
Not this flesh that covers,
Within I am a soul.

IN THE ARMS OF ETERNAL BLISS

It is not the thought of dying,
That troubles my restless mind,
But the thought of those crying,
Those I leave behind.

It is not the thought of death,
That fills me with fear,
But a prolonged death bed,
When Death draws near.

But whenever She comes,
Knocking at my door,
Whenever it's time for me,
I hope and implore,

It is not with a whimper,
Or a bang,
That I go,
But quietly in peace,
Holding her hand,
Without woe.

And never a tear, not to be missed,
In the arms of eternal bliss.

HE WHO I SEEK

He who I seek, His essence flows through the world,
He is not bound by temple walls, scriptures, within me He lives.

His Spirit lies in the seas, the forest and sky,
From the wind He calls, from every bough He gives.

His Hands are mounts, the cosmos in His palm He holds,
His heart an orb of love, with mercy He forgives.

And I am His child, born in the warm womb of faith,
Beyond this mortal life, my love for Him outlives.

WRAP YOURSELF IN A PRAYER

Sometimes when paths dim and blur,
How healing it is to surrender.
The world may scoff, mock your ways,
But how beautiful it is to bow and pray.
For no one better than Him to share,
A thousand thoughts and a million cares.
A shoulder is not strong enough,
To carry burdens with edges rough.
In every word the heart finds peace,
In every breath quiet release.
In a day, but a moment to spare,
Wrap yourself in a little prayer.

TICKLES AND GIGGLES
ON THE LIGHTER SIDE

A SMILE

A tiny tear began its journey,
Rising from the eyes,
Through dark lashes, down the cheeks,
When it heard a little sigh.
The sigh shrugged and let it go,
It never asked a why.
The little tear rolled further down
And another tear came by.
Down they rolled till a crescent curve,
A crescent that arched in style,
The tears paused when they saw,
The crescent curve a smile.
And in the dimpled deep beside,
The tears did rest a while,
Little drops of sorrow,
Now cradled in a smile.

ON LAUGHTER

Gurgling babies, chuckling kids,
Giggling teenagers on laughter grids.
A father's guffaw, a woman's tinkle,
Grandpa's grin, twinkling wrinkles.

Tears of mirth, red cheeks,
Scrunched up nose, laughter speaks.
Jiggling belly on the floor,
Chuck-le those worries out the door.

Out . . . Out . . . away with the pout.
Fumigate those tears that crowd,
Laugh a laugh, lighten a day,
Colour a heart from a sombre grey.

Laugh with some, laugh at none,
Warm, healing it's like the sun,
Smile, chuckle . . . laugh out loud,
The colour of pink hued rosy clouds.

THE GREAT INDIAN MOUSTACHE

Tucked between a flaring nose and a mouth of sparkling teeth
Lies the great Indian moustache that men so proudly keep . . . .

It could be black, a distinguished gray,
Even red or white,
The moustache is a moustache,
A rather hairy sight . . .

It could be but just a start,
All done up with care,
A phase of transition,
A light spurt of hair . . . .

It could be short, neat and trim,
That's Hitler all the way,
A face that looks rather grim,
All work and little play.

It's a matter of perspective though,
For it could make you grin,
Like the king of old comedies,
Good old Charlie Chaplin . . .
(He had his moustache,
Pretty pretty neat,
His funny little twitches,
Had us rolling at his feet).

It could be long, thick and dense,
A rather curious trend,
Resting on cushioned cheeks,
And curling at the ends.

It could of course, change its course,
And head down the chin,
Grow long and lustrous,
Like Osama Bin's . . .
A rather curious one,
I think that I do see,
Is a blob on the chin,
A beard called the goatee.

Or like a little boy's hair,
It could part in the middle,
All prim and proper,
As fit as a fiddle.

Rather useful, I would say,
For morsels and little treats,
Tuck them in the whiskers,
Then later have a feast . . .

"A sign of virility", is what men would have to say,
They'd bet on their manhood, I guess, any day,
But what makes a man a man, I think, is still kind of grey . . .
For clean-shaven men, my mustached friends, are now here to stay.

I AM A WOMAN BUT HAVE YOU HEARD ME ROAR?

So you think I am mint candy all sweet 'n nice,
Beguiled aren't you, and in for a surprise,
You feel you know me, YES, you're so sure . . .
I am a woman but have you heard me ROAR?

I am not a pot of sugar, but a barrel of SPICE,
Rub your eyes hard and think twice,
Then look the other way and don't even dare,
I may well peel you in tearful onion layers!

At your frantic antics, I am not amused,
Back off, learn, take the cues,
Better still if you just walk out that door,
Unless you'd rather stay and hear me ROAR?

Don't waste my time, don't mess around,
You won't know you; you might not be found,
One move . . . teeth will misaligned be,
In dire need of cosmetic dentistry!

Test my patience and I might swerve and start,
Push you in a corner with unknown martial arts,
I am a WOMAN. Have you NOW heard me ROAR?
Hear me clear and DON'T ask for more!

A GLASS OF WINE AND
THAT WAS IT . . . .

A glass of wine and that was it . . .
How I quipped
As lips unzipped
Oh I tipped

On the side!

A GLASS of wine and that was it . . .
Streamers red
I ripped in shreds
Screamed and said

Crimson tides!

A glass of WINE and that was it . . .
How I purred
Undeterred
Gee . . . those words

I ought to hide!

A glass of wine and THAT was it . . .
Light in the head
Whimsy led
Wisdom shed

How I smiled!

A glass of wine and that was IT . . .
So so red
Then I fled
Now in bed

Oh my pride!

A LOVER'S SOLILOQUY

He said, with ardor, that he loves me,
That his heart for my heart pines,
Of this obsession I see,
Insanely innocuous signs.
He called me his Winnie the Pooh,
His panda and his dove,
(Ought I lock myself in the zoo?
Seems I'm an animal that he loves).
He said that like an anthology,
I was an interesting read,
(He doesn't know the e of my etymology,
For I'm written all in Greek).
He said that he would be thrilled,
To have me as his wife.
(But if I were to light his kitchen,
He'd have a short shelf life).
He said that like the sky,
My eyes were blue and deep,
That my voice was a sweet lullaby . . .
(Dear me! Should I put him to sleep?).
He said that my pretty smile,
Was as wide as a well made road,
(Well, he'd have to run for miles,
Before he reached my sweet abode)

He said that I was a Wonder
Like the Great Barrier Reef,
(I sure hope he goes down-under,
I might get some reprieve.)
I think it's really not me,
That with fervour he thinks he loves,
But what he wants me to be,
For I am none of the above.
And when I am by his side,
Like a bubble I do burst,
From him, I must hide,
For he brings out my very worst.
And so my handsome lover boy,
He rants on and on,
How atrociously he annoys,
So scat, scram and begone!

TRAVEL LIGHT

She was exuberant, radiant in excitement,
A much needed holiday, a sought after break,
An odyssey, quaint locales, cuisine, new people,
Her mind in a spin, dear me, what ALL should I take?

She pulled out a dusty travel bag,
She admired it, cleaned it, preened it and vacuumed,
Wiped it with water till no dust could be spotted,
For aromatic effects sprayed a whiff of perfume.

And then began the mind mapping, the packing,
In went dresses, pairs of jeans, shirts and tees,
Woollens, stoles, loafers, flip flops, shoes,
Silk bags, belts, scarves, hats, colourful accessories.

So she packed, and she packed till she almost collapsed,
Running up and down, forever on her toes,
Content and relieved she tried to zip her bag,
Forget the zip . . . the poor bag wouldn't close.

She pulled the bag tighter together, sat on it, this way and that,
With all her force, pushed it down, from side to side,
It still wouldn't close, not even remotely so,
It sat gaping at her and grinning so wide.

Down on her knees she went, pulling, pushing the zip,
Struggling, scowling, simmering . . . what a drag,
She yanked so hard, a jerk, push, pull and push,
Off came the zip and that was the end of that!

MY HEART GOES BOOM BOODY BOOM

When he turns around to look at me,
A rainbow colours my gloom,
I dance on golden sunshine,
And my heart goes boom boody boom . . .

When he calls my name so soft,
Violins melodies croon,
Love notes are all I hear,
And my heart goes boom boody boom . . .

When he gently holds my hand,
Like a red rose fresh I bloom,
Scarlet red I beam,
And my heart goes boom boody boom . . .

Oh how I love his face,
In my heart I have him zoomed,
Like a picture he's all framed,
And I go boom boody boom boody boom . . .

Now I'll ask him to marry me,
Will he be my hunk of a groom.
I hope he says a YES,
OR he'll go boom boody, BANG BOODY BOOM!
(POOF).

SING ME A LOVE SONG BABY

Take your quill and pen some notes,
Love lyrics in melody,
Songs of passion and romance,
Write them, love, just for me.

Strike a chord, hum a note,
Give the words music sweet,
Make my heart go swayin' tappin',
Sweep me off my feet.

Then sing them baby like you do,
But sing them soft and low,
Don't pitch a note too high, my love,
For off key you do go.

Clear your throat and gargle,
Then sing a pretty tune,
Pop in a honey lemon drop,
Then smoothly you can croon.

My hearts a buzz with throbbin' romance,
But then it goes off course,
Your love notes go all awry sorry,
And you my love sound hoarse.

So sing me a love song baby,
Try not to go off key,
I'll waltz into your waitin' arms,
Love—dancin' you and me.

CRUISING A BUMPY HIGHWAY

Look the other way if you so want,
Vociferously deny it as such,
Roll your eyes and scoff,
The man does protest too much.

Chin a little higher, set stubborn,
Shoulders pulled back taut,
Brows raised in denial,
Love? Now that's a distant shot!

Shuffle your feet, cough hoarse,
Don those dark shades won't you,
Tap your fingers tra la la la,
But never say 'I do'.

Smile vacantly into space,
Back to the world with a nudge,
Who? Me? In love? No!
The man Does protest too much.

Steal occasional glances,
Then try to subtly tune,
Two worlds, yours with mine,
Aligning suns and moons.

On a roller coaster of emotions,
Down and round and above,
Deny, disagree, protest . . .
Of course you're not in love!

Hold your head and baulk,
Start at the slightest touch . . .
But never ever in love,
The man does protest too much.

Cruising the highway of love,
Everyday a rackety ride,
Fasten and tighten your seatbelt,
It's gonna be a sleepless bumpy night.

FIRST CRUSH

How well I remember my first crush,
Like it was yesterday,
How radiantly I would blush,
If he ever came my way.

How well I remember how I'd swoon,
At his comic antics,
How my silly heart would croon,
Ballads so romantic.

How well I remember my heart's flutter
As it soared like a bird,
How I would stand and stutter,
If he ever said a word.

How well I remember how I'd grin,
If he flashed a smile at me,
How I'd dance, leap and spin,
In rings of ecstasy.

Of course it was just a crush,
And nothing came of it,
But I remember the sudden rush,
And my besotted spirit.

And now at over forty years, I guess it's been a while,
But thinking of him and my poor heart still brings a smile.
A memory that in my heart, with much fondness I carry,
Even though it was his brother that I finally chose to marry.

JUST – DIAL – MOMMY

Good Morning

Welcome to MOMMY at your service.
Thank you for being on the line,
All our lines are busy at the moment,
It might take some time.
Please choose from one of the options,
And choose ONLY one,
Try not to press all buttons together,
Hang up proper once done.

If you're on the run,
Press one.
If you don't know what to do,
Press two.
If you're entangled in a tree,
Press three.
If you are locked outdoors,
Press four.
If you're holding a bee hive,
Press five.
If you've got a crick,
Press six.
If you're in a lion's den,
Press seven.
If you're in a spate,
Press eight.
If you just want to WHINE,
Press nine.

If you've been distracted,
Or haven't heard a word so far,
You may hear the options again,
Press one, two, then star.

Thank you.
Despite the incessant complaints (its not fair), the racket, the fuss,
All our callers are dearly loved, most precious to us.

MY SINGING AND MY SONGS

It was seven o' clock in the morning, so early in the day,
They came knocking at my door, they had so much to say.
At their wits end, they all sounded like a gong,
They said they had enough of it . . . my singing and my songs!

You start at four, they accused, singing notes in our ears,
Humming, then, a boomerang voice is all that we can hear.
The icing on the cake, you get the words all wrong,
They said they had enough of it, my singing and my songs!

You make a potpourri of words, then you sing off key,
Spend some time in a music class, learning do re me.
Listen to the sound of music, then try and sing along,
They said they had enough of it, my singing and my songs!

A bit of this, a bit of that, your music makes us cringe,
It's not only what you croon but also how you sing.
There's more melody in a bell, that goes but ding dong,
They said they had enough of it, my singing and my songs!

I heard them all quietly, my spirit went kapooot,
Then I thought to my self, why would I care a hoot,
Music is my world, in it I belong,
I will sing the way I like, my melody and my songs.

Gave 'em all head phones so they could drown the noise,
Cotton swabs, thick and white . . . they could block my voice.
And I started crooning, my voice clear and strong,
I will sing my heart out, though I may sound like King Kong.

SANTA WITH FAB SIX PACK ABS AND HO HO HO ...NO. NO. NO

How would Santa be,
If he were to lose all his chubby weight,
Emerge trim from the gym,
With fab six pack abs,
And a really slender waist?

His cheeks might lose their ruddy countenance,
And oh . . . their apple cherry glow,
Change diameter, radius,
color,
Become white as pallid snow.

And what of his chin, would it turn pointed, elf like,
Instead of a smooth rotund round,
Buried deep within,
His silky white beard,
Just one chin may be found.

His roly poly belly, a cushion,
Of course would then deflate,
Become hard and flat,
Off fat,
A food free empty plate.

He would not be in much danger,
Of getting stuck in the chimney I'd say,
Like a fish in water, smooth and clear,
He'll go,
Laughing all the way.

And when I'd sit on his lap (old people like to too),
I might end up with a groan,
Poked, pierced, prodded,
Bumped perhaps,
By his fat free muscles, bones.

He might not look as merry as mistletoe,
So jolly a cheerful fellow,
He might turn all sleek, svelte,
Cool,
With oomph . . . much less of a bellow.

He might not sound so delightfully robust,
His feisty zesty HO HO HO,

AND SO,
To a Santa with six pack abs,
I say a No No No No!

I like him just the way he is,
Huggable . . . in layers after layers,
But dearest Santa,
Of that beautiful heart of yours,
Do take loving care.

LITTLE CHARLIE AND SINGING IN THE SHOWER

Little Charlie loved to sing in the shower
And so loud sang he
With his yodelling tottering falsetto
He was as bad as bad could be

He sang from his heart . . . and lungs
In his little Charlie voice
Though the pitter-patter of water
Would drown some of the ignoble noise

Sometimes the neighbours could hear
A soapy sudsy note or three
But through the cascading waters
They'd have to let him be

For those who walked past
If they ever heard him sing
They would squirm, make faces
Groan, moan and cringe

A neighbour once protested
He couldn't take it anymore
But little Charlie only sang louder
Till his vocal chords turned sore

Nothing could ever stop him . . .
Hollering do re me
Oh how he loved those soapy songs
Oh how happy was he

But then who can really blame him?
From screaming, cleaning out his lungs
Squeaky shiny clean in a melody
Scrub a rub a song and done

ON PUTTING MY BEST FOOT FORWARD

I am done putting my best foot forward.
For the simple reason,
That I no longer know which one it is,
That one or this.

The left one with a meniscus torn knee,
Or the right one with a sore ankle,
That I sprained while I trained,
Myself in yoga,
But both right now,
Are irking me.

Then of course,
I am done being 'nice',
All sugar,
Little spice.
So it's time for a makeover,
A takeover, a handover.
To another I.
And to the old one,
A loud good bye.

To those who throttle and bottle my soul,
Bash and thrash my heart,
Choke and stoke my voice,
Why and fie my ways,
Suffocate and berate my mind,

You'll find,
For better or worse,
My foot right behind.

'I AM YOUR MITTEN AND YOU ARE MY GLOVE'

He spun around to look at her and said "oh my cocoa . . . my love.
I am your smitten mitten, and you, my dove, my glove."
He winked a wink at her and said, "oh my darlin' poppins,
I am your pizza and you . . . my only toppin'."

He hugged her close and kissed and said "how my heart flows"
"Aren't you a petal of the reddest reddest rose?"
He called her his sweetheart, his bunny, his pumpkin,
His honey, his muffin, his strawberry and his munchkin.

He called her his heartbeat, his only 'theme for a dream',
His chocolate, his sugar, his peaches and date ice cream,
He called her his angel, his princess, his precious queen,
He declared that she was the prettiest thing he'd ever seen.

He called her all this and all his mind could think,
Vanilla, maple syrup, a marshmallow . . . all white and pink,
Endearments he showered and he showered such love,
Birds burst into a symphony of songs from above.

How she blushed and sighed . . . the darling dear dame,
Little did she know . . . he'd forgotten her name.

DO THE 'HARLEM SHAKE', OH YEAH DO THE 'HARLEM SHAKE'

When sleep eludes on a raven night
And you are up awake
Toss those sheets on the floor
And do the Harlem shake

When you are stranded in the kitchen
And don't know what to make
Juggle the veggies in the air
And do the Harlem shake

When your face has turned beet root red
You look a summer baked
Boogie woogie through the sprinkler
And do the Harlem shake

When you are about to punch a face
And some teeth you want to break
Wriggle, jiggle your hands instead
And oh yeah, do the Harlem shake

When the going gets tough
And you get more than you can take
Get the worries going baby
Uh huh . . . . do the Harlem shake

Raise your arms in the air
Slither like a snake
Sway your hips, swing your legs
Oh, do the Harlem shake!

Yeah do the Harlem shake.

TO STRAIGHTEN OR NOT TO STRAIGHTEN, THAT IS THE QUESTION

To straighten or not to straighten the hair,
Is a question that does now impassion.
Should I let curls tumble without a care,
Or succumb to demands of quaint fashion?
Oh, how these tousled waves have triggered frowns,
Aunts, uncles, teachers their minds have spoken.
Defied mother's attempts to pin them down,
Several clips, scrunchies, bands have broken.
Mass of unruliness for long carried,
Each single strand with a mind of its own.
Hair dressers have been so alarmed, harried,
At its most unusual wild hair tone.
But it has made me who I am I say,
So what if each morn is a bad hair day?

TO EAT OR NOT TO EAT, NOW THAT IS THE QUESTION

To eat or not to eat, that is the question,
To take a slice of the scrumptious cake,
Say adieu to nagging nutrition,
And eat for satiation and desires sake.
The succulent cake to perfection done,
Lulls reservations to recline in rest,
My taste buds in a gourmet marathon,
Yearn to savour each morsel in zest.
Delectable, delicious, a devils delight,
Buttery, biscuity, bewitching, it seems,
It fills my heart, my senses, my sight,
Ooh look at the layers of luscious cream.
To eat, yes to eat, is certainly the answer,
While at it, I'll also grab a cookie hamper.

OH, THAT I WERE AN ELECTRIC KETTLE

Every morning when I am making tea,
I wish most fervently,
To become an electric KETTLE.

It most certainly won't matter to me,
I'll accept it most gracefully,
Be I of ceramic or METAL.

For one moment I'm dancing with glee,
The next sobbing mournfully,
These wretched hormones don't SETTLE.

Once I whistled so daintily,
Now I breathe so monstrously,
No longer a rose PETAL.

I may boil, then boil most furiously,
Then click off automatically,
Before I sting like NETTLE.

Splutter, bubble, gurgling I be,
Then cool and calm . . . so peacefully,
There I . . . in fine FETTLE!

A MOMMY. A PRINCESS. A FEAST FOR NAWABS

The mother made a royal feast fit for nawabs,
With starters of delicious, dreamy, creamy, succulent chicken kebabs,
A main course would follow that would make her guests sigh,
And choicest desserts . . . to delight the palate and the eye.

For hours she cooked and for hours she baked,
Then stepped into those stilettos . . . how her feet ached,
She wished she could shed legs like the skin of a snake,
Cooking, yikes, wasn't exactly a piece of chocolate cake.

Her guests she had invited very graciously before,
They had hinted they would like to come back for some more,
So she sighed and groaned but sent another polite invite,
And landed in this most wearily pitiable plight.

Well, the table she set with finery and in style,
And when they arrived, she greeted her guests with a smile,
Elegantly dressed, all with immaculate hair,
She a fine hostess, she entertained with flair.

Then came dinnertime and they settled on their chairs,
Time it was to feast but before that a little prayer,
Mommy's six-year-old princess was requested to pray,
She hesitated . . ." Oh dear mommy, what should I say?"

Someone quipped "Say what your mother said . . . perhaps yesterday."
Now words in her little head . . . there they toyed and played,
Hands folded the princess said, "Oh this will be a pain,
Dear god, why did I invite these people again?"

IT WAS A MURDER
MOST GRUESOME AND A REVENGE
MOST SWEET

And while I lay myself to sleep,
Counting lambs and little sheep,
Snuggled in a cozy bed,
I heard a buzzing in my head.

The steady drone of a mosquito,
How his music seemed to grow,
A solo for my sole ears,
One I didn't wish to hear.

He had guts I must say,
My nose he bit and there he played,
He sniggered so and oh he winked,
While my nose turned a berry pink.

As he flew past my sleepy eyes,
"Revenge, revenge "my heart cried,
Act I thought. I must be tough,
Of buzzing bites I had enough.

And so my hands I raised high,
As he puckered right to fly,
There I laid for him a trap,
Wham! Dead with a thunder clap.

And now with blood on my hands,
Fingers red with wingy strands,
Wash I must with water hot,
Out, "out damned spot".

But should SUCH critters come my way,
With vengeful valor I shall slay,
Now, however I must pray,
For "tomorrow is another day."

CHILL PILLS

Like Medusa, the Gorgon, I can turn people to stone,
Not that I've been cursed, but for my angry tone.
For better or worse, my looks can certainly kill,
And so, my daughters told me, mum, JUST take a chill pill.

This pill caught my fancy, if it would help calm me down,
(One doesn't look any prettier, in anger, with deep frowns),
So off I went to the pharmacist, right down the block,
Hoping to get my anger anchored, right in the docks.

Mr. Pharmacist, I said, I'll come straight to the point,
I haven't come to see you today for my sinus or my joints.
I have no prescription, but certain pills that I seek,
Considering it's a modern malady, I'm sure a stack you'd keep.
Give me 30 to start with, of those magical wondrous pills,
They're chill pills that I need. At times, I get FURIOUSLY ill.

He looked me up 'n down, from my head to my toes,
Through weathered glasses, on the crooked bridge of his nose.
125, 200, 500mg . . . . what potency do you need?
Is it small anger, just a flush, that you'd need to weed?
Or is it medium, that makes you see, really really red,
And you end up saying words, that you shouldn't have said?
Or is it large, kingsize, with murderous, blood shot eyes,
That you yourself become . . . . . the other's goodbye?
I pondered at the potency, the choices that I had,
I thought of all the times I'd got maddeningly mad.
I opted for all the three, my bags I did fill,
And came back home loaded with assorted chill pills.

Now in my various anger moods, I just pop one in,
And the anger metamorphoses, pops out as a grin.
No side effects, no nausea, no vomiting, I detect,
My anger is getting better, no longer I fume and fret.
(Though yesterday, a couple of times I think I may have sneezed)
Too many chill pills and my anger might freeze.

There are many in the market, just step out and choose,
I tell you . . . they're WAY BETTER than anger's nasty noose.
I'd recommend those manufactured by Laughter Incorporated,
The ones by Eccentricities Unlimited, are highly over rated,
The ones by Relaxyill, I believe are quite a fad,
For those of Meaniebeanies, I don't care a tad.
Those produced by Ah, Ah Spa, I believe are stimulating,
Though their price and packaging is rather intimidating.

But the ones made by Friends United I DO love the most,
To their bloomin' prosperous company, I propose a toast!

NOUGHT, NEVER, NAY

I see I've a head on my shoulders,
But it doesn't have a say,
For every time I turn to it,
My heart comes in the way.

When I wear a thinking cap,
The cap won't simply stay,
With all the blood being pumped about,
My heart pumps it away.

My neurons go off to lunch,
A picnic, fun filled day,
I bet my heart just coaxes them,
And declares a holiday.

I've implored my head many times,
Said, 'Hello, buddy . . . Hey!
Help me here, I need you pal!'
But to my heart, it's fallen prey.

'Tis always been this little tug,
Between my red and grey,
Can my grey ever win?
I think nought, never, nay.

ALL I WANT FOR CHRISTMAS

Wrap yourself in a little box,
With tinsel silver starlight blue,
Come knockin' at my doorstep,
All I want for Christmas is you.

Don't go a shoppin' sweetie,
Buying' me those fluorescent shoes,
Honey, your gifts are kindda different,
Shoppin' is certainly not you.

Last Christmas, I went bananas,
You gifted me a cockatoo,
It screamed away so lovingly,
And I didn't know what to do.

And before that, though very kind,
Those jars of magic glue?
To mend all the dainty porcelain,
(Accidentally) broken into smithereens by you.

Ah, those glow in dark yellow glasses,
That suddenly blocked my view,
I knocked down some friendly brethren,
And I landed in custody too.

I know you have tried . . . honey bee
Even baked me an apple stew,
So very sweet but tough.
It was to bite into.

Lovely gift givin' ideas,
Love, you've had them quite a few,
But don't go a worryin' darlin',
All I want for Christmas is you.

MADLY AND DEEPLY

It is an addiction, an affliction,
And I don't know what to do,
For I am madly and deeply,
In love with Sudoku.

It is unnerving, disturbing,
And I am going all cuckoo,
For I can't take my hands off
A game of Sudoku.

In the morning, I'm yawning,
But my fingers are all glued,
To a pen on a Daily,
Immersed in Sudoku.

An obsession, in possession,
Of numbers just a few,
Oh I can't get enough,
Of this wretched Sudoku.

One to nine, how I pine,
For the numbers in a queue,
On my phone all I see is,
A game of Sudoku.

I run late, miss my date,
In a mess through and through,
My heart full of digits.
And head of Sudoku.

An attraction, a distraction,
I sigh and sob and rue,
To be so in love,
With a game of Sudoku.

It gets worse, now a verse,
Such a long poem too!
Oh me, oh my,
All for Sudoku.

I AM NO SUPER MUM

To the world, I seem to have become,
From a mum . . . a super mum.
But after all that's said and done,
I most certainly haven't come from Krypton.

The world may laud my juggling act,
I'm both the juggler and the juggled, in fact.
And when I think of all the chores I do,
At times, I bite much more than I can chew.

Just the way I pack a lip smacking' lunch,
I can also box a motley bunch.
And if I can make some villains cower,
It's certainly not because of my super power.

It's probably just a feline instinct,
To protect my loves from becoming extinct,
Maybe, you see . . . a little brush,
With the much touted adrenalin rush.

I'm actually quite grounded, I don't fly,
I prefer the escalator, though the stairs, I try,
While I might not appear humanly sane,
I'm quite ordinary and pretty mundane.

Like the clothes I put in the washing machine,
Look at me tumble, look at me spin.
And of course, when you'll see me tumbling,
I'll be grumpy, grouchy and grumbling.
You're bound to hear me holler and shout,
Often, with my foot in the mouth.
Now, tell me, would such behaviour become,
A so-called super duper mum?

And do super beings have mood swings?
Much terror I know mine do bring . . .
As I mope in various monotones,
All because of these wretched hormones.
(And are super people supposed to cry like me,
I could probably fill up a sea.
Like the rivers of tears that flow,
Every time I watch ET or Nemo?)

Just like others, I also get tired,
Who said I was impeccably wired?
And before I run, drive and scoot,
I definitely need some time to reboot.

So,
Though I may appear to some,
A super mum I'm not, I'm just a mum.
But if you need help, just beat a drum,
Though I can't fly, huffing, puffing I'll still come.
Psst
(And the next time, you roll in the mud,
Call me too. I am all flesh and blood).

SNORING FAIRY GODMOTHERS?

What if Rapunzel had short curly hair?
And you could reach her by climbing stairs.
And if the pumpkin didn't turn into a carriage grand,
Would a Prince ever hold Cinderella's hand?
Imagine if Pinocchio's nose didn't grow,
How would Geppetto his lies ever know?
What if the three pigs and the wolf were friends?
A happy beginning, besides a happy end.
And if darling Little Red Riding Hood,
Didn't dare go singing in the woods.
What if the Mirror, Mirror on the wall,
Didn't irk the nasty Queen at all.
And if all laughter was sweet and fair,
No cackling laughter to tickle and scare.
And if a benign genie didn't rub out of a lamp,
Would Aladdin be such a heroic champ.
What if Gretel could gobble a sweet hut?
Made of candies, without a witch, so nuts.
What if there were no magic spells,
No poisoned apples, no wishing wells,
What if there were no dungeons with dragons,
Of fantasy, no unbridled bandwagons?

Wouldn't it be a tad boring?
With fairy godmothers snoring?
Interesting learns,
Through twists and turns,
Slimy, stepsisters,
Vicious, vile visitors,
Wizened, wicked witches,
Quirky, quaint glitches!

A SUNDAY AFTERNOON

A Sunday summer afternoon,
I'm not snappin' mappin',
I'm answering no calls, no foot tappin',
I'm nappin'.

Through the window, I feel the breeze,
I'm snoozin',
In my sleepy labyrinth of thoughts,
I'm cruisin'.

A beautiful day this day,
All green and blue,
The noon does beckon me,
With a clue.

A lazy, crazy,
Hazy day in June,
I turn into a bowl of jelly,
In the molten hours of noon.

No chime will alarm, declare,
It's time for lunch,
(All ye, sleep . . . do),
Wake up whenever,
You think you want to.

No cuckoo will announce,
Its time for tea,
Oh yeah, I'm dozin',
Snorin' I hope to be,

Today, I'm not caught in traffic snarls,
Nor am I rushin' through gates,
No tick tock remindin' me,
I'm runnin' late.

But before this snooze,
Before the final laze,
I must,
Walk through each room,
And handle certain hands and a face.

This afternoon,
I choose to snooze,

And I did . . .
I snoozed for long.

But this afternoon,
Somehow,
All clocks went wrong.

Whodunnit? Your guess is as good as mine,
I slept through it all . . . yeah . . . for SOMEONE,
Yes, someone 'topsy turvyed' time.

CAT WALK . . .
WALKING THE RAMP

Once, just once I walked the ramp,
And all those lights were shining on me,
When all a sudden I had a cramp,
Ouch . . . oh dear, what agony.

How I walked with a flourish and sway,
Delicate balance on heels,
But then my calf called it a day,
And oops on stage I squealed.

There I walked with a beaming smile,
With a toss of my curly mane,
One foot a time in poised style,
Then ouch . . . I squirmed in pain.

Oh I walked with a look so crisp,
Then my leg just hung up there,
Cramps across like a needling whip,
How I longed for a chair.

Oh I walked with zest and zeal,
My chin all aligned in grace,
But then the cramps, the stiletto heel,
Ouch . . . I fell on my face.

How I walked with my nose all up,
A showstopper I wanted to be,
But then this fall from lofty heights,
The show stopped because of me.

THE LADY IS A TRAMP

The lady is a tramp and she doesn't care a hoot,
For Gucci, Nina Ricci, or them designer boots,
She dons a large tunic, big enough for two,
A yellow purple shirt, with scarlet orange shoes.

Her hair is unruly, not a strand I can tame,
Sun kissed and wind tousled, her defiant mane,
Her eyes are fiery green and oh how she winks,
Her cheeks sunset red, and lips a dancin' pink.

The lady is a tramp, the lady all wild,
M'lady is a woman, m' lady a child.
No mincin' words, she speaks out her mind,
The lady is a tramp and one of a kind.

No grooming school can ever set her right,
Always on her heels, she is ready for flight,
She goes to my head, a glass of summer wine,
The lady is a tramp, but yes, she is mine.

Starry eyed I follow her, wherever she goes,
Right behind my only love . . . as the wind blows,
Sleeping on the streets, merry' in the gutter,
I her man and she my cocoa butter.

No riches, no land, but yet I am a czar,
She for me, I for her, lookin' up at the stars.

MOLTEN MOMENTS

Chocolate silk,
Satin smooth,
Every bite,
Melts within.

Finger licking,
Temptation,
But a touch,
I give in.

Scent a taste,
Fills the head,
Feel the senses,
Reel and spin.

But a glimpse,
Turn on mood,
All cream 'n soft,
I begin.

Sweet trail,
On the lips,
On laughter lines,
Almond skin.

Oh, some more,
The heart pleads,
And there I sink,
In chocolate whim.

MY HEART . . . A – DANCIN' IT GOES

Every time I'm ecstatic, for reasons I don't know,
Lights flash in my heart and it kind of . . . . discos.

Why not a waltz, polka, salsa, jive, tango or calypso,
Of all dances, I am not sure why it chooses to disco.

(Maybe, 'tis a dance that it can dance on it's own,
A dance in merry solitude when I might be alone . . . .)

Maybe, I grew up in that era when Saturday Night Fever was in tow,
When pop charts went tizzy with songs that'd make
the world boom boom go.

Maybe, my heart beats to the rhythm of life, at times funky . . .
at times slow
Maybe, it's in tune with electronic sounds around me
that in a humdrum flow.

The top left chamber of my heart, leaps, jumps and thumps so,
The bottom right chamber shakes a leg with a psychedelic lights show.

My arteries and ventricles throb and pulsate oh . . . OH!
Pumping blood in a sudden rush all the way to my toes.

And like the ever-glittering disco ball, I glisten, radiate and glow,
Every time I'm happy, my heart jumps . . . n' a dancin' it goes.

AN AFTERWORD

I would like to thank my family for their continuous support, patience and encouragement. As a poet, there is a strong inclination to dream night and day so thank you for putting up with my distant, far away and lost look. A thank you to my parents for fostering these creative impulses I had as a child and those dinnertime couplets that I believe helped me fall in love with rhyme. A thank you especially to my daughters for listening to me spout poetry. (I forgive the incessant rolling of the eyes). To have a poet as a mother, I believe, is one of life's challenges!

I would also like to thank my extended family of co poets and friends. Without their constant appreciation and feedback, this book would not have happened. Thank you to these many wonderful 'voices' that have so patiently heard what I had to say.

A very special thanks to Sita Narayan for her beautiful illustration of the cover page and the talented sketches that have added another dimension to my work.
Love you all!